OLD TESTAMENT GUIDES

General Editor

R.N. Whybray

JEREMIAH

JEREMIAH

R. P. Carroll

Published by JSOT Press
for the Society for Old Testament Study

For a generation of university students who have tried to understand me trying to understand the book of Jeremiah!

Schools and universities ought to help us to understand that no book that talks *about* a book says more than the book in question.
Italo Calvino

Copyright © 1989 Sheffield Academic Press

Published by JSOT Press
JSOT Press is an imprint of
Sheffield Academic Press Ltd
The University of Sheffield
343 Fulwood Road
Sheffield S10 3BP
England

Typeset by Sheffield Academic Press
and
printed in Great Britain
by A. Wheaton & Co. Ltd
Exeter

British Library Cataloguing in Publication Data

Carroll, Robert P.
    Jeremiah.
    1. Bible. O.T. Jeremiah
    I. Title   II. Series
    222′50924

    ISBN 1-85075-146-3

CONTENTS

PREFACE

After I had delivered the typescript of my OTL commentary on Jeremiah to its publisher I went down to Cambridge for the Summer meeting of SOTS (1985). There at some point during the proceedings Professor Whybray asked me if I would write the JSOT Guide to Jeremiah. A brief silence ensued while both of us expected a polite refusal as the appropriate response to this question. To our, I suspect, mutual surprise the answer heard was 'yes'! I certainly was surprised to be asked and even more surprised to have agreed to undertake the task. After having written so long a book on Jeremiah, horse sense should have warned me to avoid the even more difficult task of writing a short book on the same subject. I thank Professor Whybray for the kind invitation and, above all, for his tolerance and *patience* shown towards my efforts in this direction. Having taught university students over the past twenty years the text of Jeremiah I still find the book a most elusive piece of literature, and the quest of understanding it baffles me to this day. But from the grotesque length of the commentary to the absurd brevity of this book that quest goes on, because it is not given to human beings to desist from that search for understanding.

Robert P. Carroll
University of Glasgow
Christmas 1987

ABBREVIATIONS

BCE	Before the Common Era
BETL	Bibliotheca Ephemeridum Theologicarum Lovaniensium
BHS	Biblia Hebraica Stuttgartensia
BZAW	Beihefte zur *Zeitschrift für die alttestamentliche Wissenschaft*
CE	The Common Era
ET	English translation
EVV	English Versions (of the Bible)
FRLANT	Forschungen zur Religion und Literatur des Alten und Neuen Testaments (Vandenhoeck & Ruprecht, Göttingen)
ICC	The International Critical Commentary
JBL	*Journal of Biblical Literature*
JNES	*Journal of Near Eastern Studies*
JSOT	*Journal for the Study of the Old Testament*
JSOTS	Journal for the Study of the Old Testament Supplement Series
LXX	Septuagint (Greek translation of Hebrew Bible)
MT	Masoretic Text (standard edition of Hebrew Bible)
OAN	Oracles against the nations
OTL	Old Testament Library
RSV	Revised Standard Version
SBLDS	Society of Biblical Literature Dissertation Series
SVT	Supplements to *VT*
VT	*Vetus Testamentum*
WMANT	Wissenschaftliche Monographien zum Alten und Neuen Testament
ZAW	*Zeitschrift für die alttestamentliche Wissenschaft*

1

INTRODUCTION: ARGUING ABOUT JEREMIAH

THE BOOK OF JEREMIAH is long, complex, and difficult. To the modern reader it appears to be a repetitive mess, a mixture of poetry and prose, in no particular order, but containing traces of attempts to collate and give some order to parts of the material. A cacophony of voices is heard in the book, which makes it all the more difficult to accept the single attribution of the work to one man in 1.1. The reader who is not confused by reading the book of Jeremiah has not understood it! These initial problems of reading also exist for the scholars who have studied the book and written about it. As a book Jeremiah remains enigmatic in many ways for the scholar, like so much else in the Bible. Every aspect of the book is controversial and much of modern scholarship on Jeremiah consists of disputes and arguments about its meaning and how it came into existence. This highly argumentative scrutiny of the book is very much due to its present shape, the difficulty of understanding the relation of the different parts of the book to each other, and the entire absence of firm knowledge about the book's origins. It is important at the outset of studying the book of Jeremiah to be aware of just how much scholars *do not know* about the early history and formation of the book. This high degree of ignorance (nescience is a good technical word which should be heard more frequently from scholars!) is at the root of all the arguing about Jeremiah. Argument is of course the lifeblood of scholarship and, even if we knew everything about the origins of the book, would persist in terms of the meaning of the text. But knowing nothing about the formation of Jeremiah scholars must generate hypotheses about its origins, and all such theoretical constructions are bound to be the subject of fierce arguments by other scholars supporting different hypotheses. Thus argument is the essence of reading Jeremiah.

We do not know when Jeremiah first came into existence as a book, though we do know that at Qumran (the area beside the Dead Sea where the famous scrolls were located in 1947) traces have been found of at least two different editions of the book. From these fragments of text we may deduce that Jeremiah existed in writing by the mid-second century BCE, but that it had no *one fixed form of the text*. To speculate on the basis of the Qumran evidence when either of these textual traditions *first* came into existence would be foolish. Other information from outside the book of Jeremiah is extremely scant: Jeremiah is mentioned in 2 Chron. 35.25 as having uttered a lament for king Josiah, but nothing resembling this lament appears in Jeremiah (quite the contrary according to 22.10-11!); 2 Chron. 36.12 might be regarded as a summary of Jer. 37–38 and v. 21 an interpretation of the reference to 'seventy years' in Jer. 25.11-12 *or* 29.10. 2 Chron. 36.22 (= Ezra 1.1) refers to Jeremiah's word but nothing specific is cited, and what follows does not match anything in the book of Jeremiah. Dan. 9.2 also refers to the 'seventy years' which Daniel 'perceived *in the books*' and mentions Jeremiah. Now the book of Daniel may be dated to the mid-second century BCE (about the same time as the Qumran community), whereas Chronicles is much more difficult to date (perhaps fourth–third centuries BCE, but parts might be earlier or later!), so the only biblical evidence for the existence of the book of Jeremiah is probably no earlier than 300 BCE. Of course the book may have existed in various forms before then, but we have absolutely no evidence to indicate when or in what forms. It should also be recognized that the references in Daniel and Chronicles do not constitute evidence of the form or extent of the book, citing as they do material from 29.10-14 and conceivably 38.17. Ben Sira in his reference to Jeremiah alludes to the firing of the city and also to information contained in Jer. 1.5, 10 (Ecclus 49.6-7), but this also is a book from the second century BCE.

The information contained in 1.1-3 tells us nothing about when the book was written or by whom. It simply specifies the identity of the speaker as Jeremiah, son of Hilkiah, of the priests of Anathoth, and assigns the period of his preaching to the closing decades of life in pre-exilic Jerusalem (c. 626-587 BCE). This then is the period in which the editors would have us place Jeremiah, but it certainly does not follow that the book was written at that time. Nor need it be supposed that the editorial setting of the book necessarily reflects any reliable historical information. The precise status of 1.1-3 in relation to the book which follows is much debated among scholars, and there is no evidence external to the book which would corroborate any particular theory. It may well be the case that the colophon of 1.1-3 is a fictional creation of the editors which may (or may not) reflect traditional beliefs about the book; or it may be an imaginary setting necessary for understanding what follows. The conventions governing the colophons to the biblical books (where there are any) are unknown to us, so we cannot be definite about what is entailed by statements such as 1.1-3. But allowance should be made for editorial creativity: e.g. it is not possible to appreciate fully Tom Stoppard's play *Rosencrantz and Guildenstern are Dead* without knowing that it takes place in and around the time of Shakespeare's *Hamlet*, but it would be extremely foolish to insist that both plays relate in some literal sense to the real Denmark, Elsinore and Amled. We know and understand the conventions governing drama, even when real names and places are involved; we do not know the conventions of the biblical writers and therefore may not assume that there are inevitably historical connections between setting and text. The book of Jeremiah may be read in the light of 1.1-3 without the reader's having to assume that it is more than a summary extracted from the book itself or a conventional setting for it.

If argument is of the essence when reading Jeremiah then it must be admitted that, while the facts set out in the above paragraphs are indisputably correct, the interpretation put on those facts will be disputed by many scholars. Biblical scholarship is very tradition-bound and follows traditional beliefs while developing new and better arguments to support such beliefs. Thus many scholars accept as axiomatic that the words of Jeremiah represented in the book of Jeremiah are indeed the words of the historical Jeremiah who worked in Jerusalem from at least 626 to 587 BCE and even beyond then. Some editorial control is allowed for, varying in degree from scholar to scholar, but by and large many researchers on Jeremiah insist on a very close connection between the book and the 'historical' Jeremiah. If I put the word 'historical' within inverted commas it is to indicate to the reader that we are dealing with a disputed and questionable concept. Here is one centre of argument in Jeremiah studies, one which might loosely be called 'the quest of the historical Jeremiah', thus signalling affinities with New Testament scholarship's debate about the historical Jesus. It would be easy to get involved in the arguments about the relation of the book to the real Jeremiah of history (of whom we only know from the book itself!); but here I only wish to inform the reader that there is a central problem of interpretation which cannot be resolved by scholarly diktat. Axiomatic assertions such as that the poetry must have been spoken by somebody and that in view of 1.1-3 that somebody must have been Jeremiah are really very unhelpful. It is not unreasonable to accept, for the sake of argument, that the book purports to be the work of a fictional character called Jeremiah and then to proceed from that point to treat the work *as if* such a figure behaved and spoke in the ways attributed to him in the book. We would understand Odysseus (Homer), Macbeth (Shakespeare), Lemuel Gulliver (Swift), or Leopold Bloom (Joyce) in such ways, and there is no good reason to treat biblical characters in a different fashion. What we would not do is to insist on a one-to-one correspondence between the fictional characters and any historical counterparts we might imagine of them (e.g. the Scottish king Macbeth or the models used by Joyce for Bloom). A similar approach must be advocated for reading Jeremiah. We should treat the character of Jeremiah as a work of fiction and recognize the impossibility of moving from the book to the real 'historical' Jeremiah, given our complete lack of knowledge independent of the book itself.

The argumentative approach to Jeremiah cannot be avoided once any two books on the subject are investigated. Each book reads the text in a different way and makes different assumptions about that text as a total entity and about the factors which produced it. One approach may insist on reading the book chronologically, assigning to every statement in it a time and place of origin; another reading of it may insist on how little can be known about the book in the first place and therefore refuse to read it chronologically. Between these two approaches will be many which concede something to each but which maintain a different balance between chronology and undatable pieces of text. But what if the chronological information is derivable from the editing of the book by its producers? What do we know about the book's editors? Nothing! Unlike some Babylonian cuneiform literature which gives information about its writers, the Bible does not indicate who *wrote* what. So any positing of editors is theoretical, a hypothesis to account for the transformation of words into literature and for the continued transmission of such literary works down through the ages. But such an hypothesis is a necessary one. Any information about such hypothesized writers will have to be gleaned inferentially from the transmitted writings; and such gleanings may be very sparse, as editors seldom edit themselves into their texts (is Jer. 36 an exception?).

The arguments could be developed much further than space permits; but always they would come up against our profound ignorance of the facts and production values in the creation of the book of Jeremiah. Argument and ignorance are the twin emphases of the present book's approach to reading Jeremiah. This stress on ignorance may be in marked contrast to many of the books recommended for the study of Jeremiah, books which very confidently assert as fact what is, at best, only assumption. Such a contrast should be noted as being, perhaps, out of sympathy with traditionalist approaches to reading Jeremiah, but it should also be recognized as working with fewer basic assumptions than is usually the case in biblical studies. A reading of various authors on Jeremiah will provide a balanced diet and redress any danger of imbalance produced by following the argument of this introduction to Jeremiah studies. What this book is intended to do is very simple: accompany the reader on a journey through the book of Jeremiah, assuming a familiarity with that book in the first place (in other words, read the book of Jeremiah a few times before reading this book once!), and pointing out the landmarks of interpretation. Because this is necessarily a short book it will not be possible to pursue any argument fully to its logical conclusions. It is also improbable that the full extent of every major scholar's work on Jeremiah can be set forth or the subtleties of the text itself comprehensively displayed. Jeremiah is a large book and full of intricate wordplays in the Hebrew; no English translation of it will do it justice and no commentary on it can hope to be comprehensive. A short introduction will therefore barely scrape the surface of this complex book. This means that a great deal of the book's contents may only appear in passing, and only a few pieces of text will be focused on in relation to interpretative problems.

The imbalance of large-scale biblical book and small introductory guide is how these things ought to be. It preserves the proportions of significance and reminds the reader that in this particular enterprise the point of the exercise is to enable the reading of the text rather than the hearing of opinions. Once the text is mastered (!) there will be time for the reading of commentaries and all the secondary literature which will, in their own way, prove to be as difficult to understand as is the original text! The only assumption I have made in writing this book is that the reader knows the text of Jeremiah very well and is capable of moving back and forward through the text so as to follow the cross-referential approach to it taken here. A knowledge of the RSV is assumed because that is the English version used throughout this guide, but those who also have Hebrew, Greek, French, and German will find the secondary literature equally accessible. I happen to think that 'the necessity of interpretation' is fundamentally important as an approach to the Bible, but I also recognize that reading the text itself, without benefit of commentary or guide, can be a most salutary experience and a brain-sizzling event for any reader. I would therefore conclude this introduction by citing the full quotation from Italo Calvino, of which only part of one sentence forms the epithet to this book:

> The reading of a classic ought to give us a surprise or two vis-à-vis the notion that we had of it. For this reason, I can never sufficiently highly recommend the direct reading of the text itself, leaving aside the critical biography, commentaries, and interpretations as much as possible. Schools and universities ought to help us understand that no book that talks *about* a book says more than the book in question, but instead they do their level best to make us think the opposite. There is a widespread topsy-turviness of values whereby the introduction, critical apparatus, and bibliography are used as a smokescreen to hide what the text has to say and, indeed, can say only if left to speak for itself without intermediaries who claim to know more then the text does.

Further Reading

The citation of Calvino (and the epithet) is from his essay 'Why Read the Classics?', in *The Literature Machine: Essays*, London: Secker & Warburg, 1987, 128-29. Arguments about Jeremiah will be found in the introductions to commentaries and in reviews of books on Jeremiah as well as in the monographs mentioned in the Further Reading sections of this book; see in particular:

J.M. Berridge, *Prophet, People, and the Word of Yahweh: An Examination of Form and Content in the Proclamation of the Prophet Jeremiah* (Basel Studies in Theology 4), Zurich: EVZ-Verlag, 1970.

R.P. Carroll, *From Chaos to Covenant: Uses of Prophecy in the Book of Jeremiah*, London: SCM Press, 1981. *idem, Jeremiah*, 33-86.

W. McKane, *Jeremiah* 1, xli-xcix

J. Skinner, *Prophecy and Religion: Studies in the Life of Jeremiah*, Cambridge: Cambridge University Press, 1922.

Two excellent collections of essays on aspects of Jeremiah studies are:

P.-M. Bogaert (ed.), *Le livre de Jérémie: Le prophète et son milieu, les oracles et leur transmission* (BETL 54), Leuven: Leuven University Press, 1981 (cited as Bogaert).

L.G. Perdue & B.W. Kovacs (eds.), *A Prophet to the Nations: Essays in Jeremiah Studies*, Winona Lake: Eisenbrauns, 1984 (cited as Perdue & Kovacs).

Good introductory survey essays on the arguments about the book of Jeremiah are:

J.L. Crenshaw, 'A Living Tradition: The Book of Jeremiah in Current Research', *Interpretation* 37, 1983, 117-29.

L.G. Perdue, 'Jeremiah in Modern Research: Approaches and Issues', in Perdue & Kovacs, 1-32.

There are many general books on the Hebrew Bible which devote a chapter to Jeremiah and some of these are well worth consulting, e.g.:

W. Brueggemann, *Hopeful Imagination: Prophetic Voices in Exile*, Philadelphia: Fortress Press, 1986, part 1, 9-47.

J.L. Crenshaw, *A Whirlpool of Torment: Israelite Traditions of God as an Oppressive Presence* (Overtures to Biblical Theology 12), Philadelphia: Fortress Press, 1984, ch. 2, 31-56.

Essential reading for the background to Jeremiah is:

P.R. Ackroyd, *Exile and Restoration: A Study of Hebrew Thought of the Sixth Century BC* (OTL), London: SCM Press, 1968.

For the general religious background to Jeremiah assumed in this book see:

M. Barker, *The Older Testament: The Survival of Themes from the Ancient Royal Cult in Sectarian Judaism and Early Christianity*, London: SPCK, 1987.

G. Garbini, *History & Ideology in Ancient Israel*, London: SCM Press, 1988.

M. Smith, *Palestinian Parties and Politics that Shaped the Old Testament*, 2nd edn, London: SCM Press, 1987.

2

CONTENTS AND
STRUCTURE
OF THE BOOK

A STRUCTURE IS DISCERNIBLE in the book of Jeremiah which, though debated by scholars as to its precise details, may usefully be drawn to the attention of the reader as a way of organizing the large amount of loosely shaped material into blocks of more easily categorized sections. In attempting to divide a book as large as Jeremiah into large blocks and smaller sub-sections the analyst soon begins to grasp the difficulty of the task and to understand how complex is the material gathered together in this one book. Furthermore, the attempt to categorize the parts and sections by title or description or to justify the precise divisions made soon raises many questions of definition and understanding which in themselves help to further comprehension of the task facing the interpreter of the book of Jeremiah. Each section or description of that section may be disputed as to extent of division or accuracy of the summary of its contents. Every reader will offer a different assessment of the contents of a section, and in some cases there will be disagreement about the precise point where a block may begin or end (e.g. ch. 36 as the end of part III or the beginning of the next part). Yet the individual attempt at spelling out the contents of Jeremiah is worth making, if only as a voyage of discovery of the complexities of the book and for the tantalizing convenience of a structured pattern to what often looks like a haphazard collection of disjunctive pieces of text. In conjunction with what follows the reader is well advised to read through the text of Jeremiah a number of times in order to become familiar with its contents, and only to use my structuring of the book as a convenient guide rather than as a word from Sinai!

Prologue: 1.1-19

1.1-3: editorial colophon introducing the speaker, his family and social location, and the time of his activity; 4-10: poem of commissioning as a prophet to the nations; 11-14: two visions; 15-16, 17-19: additional material.

Part I: 2.1–25.14 Poems and sermons against Judah and Jerusalem

A. 2.1–6.30
2.1-3: preface to the cycles of poetry in A; 2.4–4.4: discursive poems, with prose elements, on false cultic attitudes; 4.5–6.26: cycle of poems on 'the foe from the north' and other themes; 6.27-30: coda.

B. 7.1–10.25
7.1–8.3: sermons against cultic practices; 8.4–9.26: collection of discrete poems; 10.1-16: polemic against idols and hymn to Yahweh; 10.17-25: independent fragments.

C. 11.1–13.27
11.1-14: the preacher of the covenant; 11.15–12.13: various poems and laments; 12.14-17: prose fragment about the nations; 13.1-11: the waistcloth incident with interpretation; 13.12-14: sayings about a jar of wine; 13.15-27: sundry poems.

D. 14.1–17.27
14.1–15.4: a cycle of poems and prose loosely associated with a drought; 15.5-21: poems, laments, fragments of prose; 16.1-9: sermon against social gatherings of the people; 16.10–17.18: miscellany of poetry and prose; 17.19-27: rulings about the sabbath.

E. 18.1–20.18
18.1-12: Jeremiah at the potter's house; 18.13-17: poem about apostasy; 18.18: prose fragment; 18.19-23: a lament; 19.1–20.6: incident with ceramic flask, sermon against fire-cult and false gods, and matters arising; 20.7-18 laments.

F. 21.1–24.10 Appendix to Part I
21.1-10: Zedekiah and the fate of Jerusalem and its people; 21.11–23.6: cycle of poems and prose about the house of David and the city;

23.7-8: oracle of restoration; 23.9-40: cycle of poems and prose concerning the prophets; 24.1-10: vision of two baskets of figs with complex explanation. Summary of Part I: 25.1-14

Part II: 25.15-38; 46-51
Oracles against the nations (OAN)

25.15-29: incident with wine cup, list of nations; 25.30-38 poetic denunciation of the nations; 46.1: title introducing OAN; 46.2-26: poems against Egypt; 46.27-28: restoration of Israel; 47.1-7 : against the Philistines; 48.1-47: poetic and prose denunciations of Moab; 49.1-6: against the Ammonites; 49.7-22: against Edom; 49.23-27: against Damascus; 49.28-33: against Kedar and the kingdoms of Hazor; 49.34-39: against Elam; 40.1-51, 58: poems and prose denouncing Babylon; 51.59-64: incident with a book against Babylon.

Part III: 26-36 Miscellaneous narratives and cycles

26: Jeremiah before the 'tribunal'; 27-29: independent cycle of material against prophets; 30.1-31.22: cycle of poems of restoration; 31.23-33.26: prose additions to the cycle; 34.1-7: Jeremiah speaks to Zedekiah; 34.8-22: emancipation of the slaves and a sermon; 35: incident with the Rechabites and sermon; 36: the writing of a scroll and its various readings.

Part IV: 37-45 The fall of Jerusalem and aftermath

37.1-2: titular summary; 37.3-38.28: Jeremiah during the siege of Jerusalem; 39.1-10: the fall of Jerusalem; 39.11-14: the release of Jeremiah; 39.15-18: words to Ebed-Melech; 40.1-6: release of Jeremiah; 40.7-41.18: Gedaliah's governorship and assassination; 42.1-6: communal appeal to Jeremiah; 42.7-22: sermon against flight to Egypt; 43.1-7: response to sermon and retreat to Egypt; 43.8-13: incident in Egypt; 44: denunciations against the Jewish communities in Egypt, with responses; 45: lament of Baruch with oracular response.

Epilogue: 52.1-34 (cf. 2 Kings 24.18-25.30)

52.1-3a: summary of Zedekiah's rule; 52.3b-11: fall of Jerusalem and

Zedekiah's fate; 52.12-16: destruction of Jerusalem and deportation; 52.17-23: transportation of temple furnishings; 52.24-27: execution of leading citizens; 52.28-30: statistics of three deportations; 52.31-34: release of Jehoiachin from prison.

3

EDITIONS OF JEREMIAH

TO THE ORDINARY READER of the book of Jeremiah there is only one such book, so I must explain what is meant by the phrase 'editions of Jeremiah'. It is always a mistake to imagine that anything to do with the Bible is simple; and in the case of Jeremiah the matter is especially complex. What we have are two editions of the book of Jeremiah: one in Hebrew and one in Greek, i.e. one represented by the Masoretic Text (MT), the basis of the translation in English Bibles, and one represented by the Septuagint (LXX). The differences between the two versions are such that it is reasonable to think of the two linguistic traditions as representing distinctive editions of the book of Jeremiah. Fragments of both editions have been found at Qumran, so at least until the second century BCE there was no fixed or unified text of the book of Jeremiah. The Greek edition is a shorter version of the book which, via the Hebrew, appears in English Bibles, and yet the LXX elsewhere normally has an expanded account of the MT, so its comparative brevity here is remarkable and noteworthy. It also has a different arrangement of some of the chapters and a tendency not to have so many repeated textual units as the MT. What it may represent is the translation into Greek of an earlier Hebrew version of Jeremiah than the present MT text. This earlier Hebrew text may either be lost or now incorporated into the expanded MT version, so that it may be possible to compare the two versions and determine what have been the essential developments of the book between the editions. The longer Hebrew text is probably best regarded as constituting a second, or expanded, edition of the *Vorlage* (underlying or parent text) behind the Greek translation. It is this distinction between the two editions of Jeremiah which makes the study of *both* versions an important aspect of the interpretation of the book.

Greek edition (LXX)

The study of the Greek text of the book of Jeremiah is a very complex and technical field of study, perhaps wisely left to linguistic experts at home in the scrutiny of multiple families of texts, and capable of sensitive judgment of different readings in terms of their relative values, and alert to the subtleties of retroversion (the translation of a text back into its parent language, i.e. Greek into Hebrew). This is a new area of growth in modern biblical studies, and the less than scholarly are advised to stay well away from the pitfalls of retroversion and multiple textual readings. A glance at the critical apparatus to Joseph Ziegler's edition of the LXX Jeremiah will indicate something of the formal complexities of that text.

The most striking difference between the LXX and the MT versions of Jeremiah is the shorter text represented by the Greek: it is about one-seventh shorter; and this, in a book of fifty-two chapters, is a considerable degree of difference. That proportion (14.7%) of variation between the two editions is not represented by fewer chapters but by fewer words and verses in the Greek (some 3,097 words in MT are not in LXX, whereas LXX has some 307 words not found in MT). Working from these figures it is clear that the second edition of Jeremiah (MT) was developed by a process of expansion whereby additional words, phrases and verses filled out the shorter text and gave it a number of different nuances. There is in the LXX a tendency for the epithets used to qualify the deity to be fewer and briefer than in the MT, and this variation may point in the direction of a theological or liturgical development of the Hebrew edition represented by the MT. A further important difference between the two editions reflected by the LXX is the latter's distinctive arrangement of the oracles against the nations (OAN). In the Greek these are to be found in chs. 26–32, following on from the conclusion of part I in 25.1-13 and logically associating all the OAN material together. In the MT the initial listing of the nations in 25.15-38 (LXX 32) is not followed by the OAN but by parts III and IV, and the OAN appear in 46–51. The order of the OAN is also different in the two editions. So the distinctive placements of the OAN in the two editions indicate different editorial policies on the part of the editors of each tradition. Beyond that factual observation it is rather difficult to determine the reasons for the different locations of the OAN.

Hebrew edition (MT)

Contrary to normal expectations the MT of Jeremiah is longer than the edition represented by the LXX—throughout the Hebrew Bible, with very few exceptions, the LXX is an expansionary translation. The minuses of the Greek or the pluses of the Hebrew (the perspective is relative!) may be observed in 8.10-12; 10.6-8; 11.7-8; 17.1-5; 23.36-37 by those prepared to do a comparative study of LXX, MT, and the English translations. In 27.18-22 the longer MT (LXX 34.15-18) is not only a considerably developed text but what is additional changes something of the meaning of the passage in its context. 33.14-26; 39.4-13 do not appear in the LXX. Some of the repetitions of the MT may be indicative of editorial expansion of the text, suggesting a high degree of editorial construction of the tradition without revealing any clear reasons why pieces are repeated in the book. The MT has a tendency to expand the epithets used of the deity much more than does the LXX: e.g. 'Yahweh *of hosts, the god of Israel*' (35.13) appears in LXX simply as *kurios* 'lord' (42.13), as is the case in vv. 17, 18 (v. 19a of MT is not in LXX). Development between the editions here may reflect pious glossing of the text in the context of theological or liturgical reflection and usage. The accumulation of so many small qualifiers and expansions contributes substantially to the larger Hebrew edition of Jeremiah without seriously altering its significance.

One development between the two editions may be noted here: the phrase 'Jeremiah *the prophet*' (*hannābî'*) only appears in the LXX four times (42/49.2; 43/50.6; 45.1/51.31; 51/28.59 EVV references first), whereas in the second edition there are a further twenty-six references to Jeremiah as *the prophet* (20.2; 25.2; 28.5, 6, 10, 11, 12, 15; 29.1; 32.2; 34.6; 36.8, 26; 37.2, 3, 6, 13; 38.9, 10, 14; 42.4; 46.1, 13; 49.34; 50.1)! Such a six-fold increase may be regarded as significant and as pointing to the direction in which the Jeremiah story developed between the editions. LXX seems to know Jeremiah as a prophet only after the fall of Jerusalem; and this may reflect the characterization of Jeremiah as a 'prophet to the nations' (1.5). In the second edition his designation as 'the prophet' is so frequently used that in the book he now becomes the prophet *par excellence*! Whether this signifies more than the logical development of the tradition is a matter for reflection and debate. Two other features of the Hebrew edition may be noted: there is a high degree of wordplay in the book of Jeremiah which cannot always be represented in English translations (e.g. 2.8b; 8.4; 22.22), and the MT has a high level of variant readings of the text represented by the technical terms *Ketîb-Qerê* (what is written but what should be read and vice versa). Such marginal corrections of the text by the masoretes (from which the MT derives its name) indicate that variation and interpretation are built into the Hebrew text as well as existing between the editions, and make the Jeremiah tradition a rather complex one.

Deuteronomistic edition
On a different level, more hypothetical too, some scholars argue for various editions within the book of Jeremiah which may be regarded as stages in the growth and development of the tradition. The most notable of these is the deuteronomistic edition of Jeremiah. The presence of such an edition is deduced from a number of lengthy prose passages in Jeremiah which display a similarity of style, language and thought to such biblical books as Deuteronomy and the so-called (by many scholars) Deuteronomistic History detected in Joshua–Judges–Samuel–Kings. This family resemblance between different writings suggests that one element in the construction of the book of Jeremiah was the work of that circle of writers who were responsible for producing Deuteronomy and for preparing an edition of the story of Israel from its settlement in the land to the Babylonian conquest of Jerusalem. The contributions of this circle to the creation of the Jeremiah tradition may be seen especially in 7.1–8.3; 11.1-17; 13.1-11; 14.1–15.4; 16.1-13; 17.19-27; 18.7-12; 19.1–20.6; 21.1-12; 22.1-5; 24; 25.1-13a; 26; 27; 29.10-20; 32; 33.1-13; 34.8-22; 35.12-19; 36.28-31; 37.1-2; 39–40.1-6; 42.7-22; 44; 45 (following Hyatt's listing). There are also many individual short units and verses which have been added to the text by the deuteronomistic editors (e.g. 1.15-16, 18-19; 3.6-14; 5.18-19; 8.19b; 17.2b-3a). The two main features provided by this editorial process would appear to be the creation of a number of sermons and stories in which the prophet Jeremiah reflected on the people's way of life in accordance with deuteronomistic ideology, and the numerous adjustments of poems and texts with clichés typical of deuteronomistic thought.

The most thoroughgoing analysis of the book of Jeremiah from the perspective of a deuteronomistic edition is that by Winfried Thiel, whose two-volume work is an exhaustive consideration of the range, techniques and purpose displayed by the deuteronomists in their supplementation of Jeremiah. It should be noted, however, that not all scholars see the hand of deuteronomistic editors in the many prose passages of chs. 1–45, and rather different explanations are offered by various writers on the subject (see Chapter 4). As a theory the notion of a deuteronomistic edition of Jeremiah has much explanatory value, but like all hypotheses it is subject to serious dispute by scholars who believe the data to be capable of being explained in rather different ways. Some would argue that such prose is typical of normal seventh-century (BCE) speech patterns and would accordingly attribute the sermons to Jeremiah. Such a line of argument would deny the existence of a deuteronomistic edition of Jeremiah altogether; and therefore this element of Jeremiah studies belongs as much to disputes about the formation and interpretation of the book as it does to a section on editions of Jeremiah. Whatever judgment is made in this matter it is important to recognize that allowance should also be made for the existence of a fair amount of post-deuteronomistic material in Jeremiah (e.g. 18.7-9; 31.31-34). Controversy is likely to remain a dominant feature of discussions about these elements in the prose of Jeremiah as there are no objective criteria available to control the arguments advanced by individual scholars.

The editorial framework
Without substantial editing we should not possess any biblical book in the first place! Who these editors were or who transmitted the written texts down through the centuries we do not know. They are all anonymous, but that fact should not blind the reader to their existence. The book of Jeremiah as we know it shows many traces of such editing, especially in the different arrangements of blocks of material by the Greek and Hebrew editions, and clearly owes its present shape to much editorial construction. In spite of the many discrete, disparate and even disjunctive pieces constituting the book it is held together by a complex editorial framework which, at times, gives it some appearance of coherence and direction. The introductory colophon of 1.1-3 provides information, whatever its historical reliability may be, without which it would be difficult to understand the book. It gives the tradition a setting in a particular period and provides some identification of the speaker credited with the words

in the book. Even though it is a secondary and editorial statement, it is a very necessary piece of writing which brings some order to what otherwise would be a jumbled collection of words. Whether it reflects a genuine tradition about the speaker behind the text, is a legendary belief picked up by the editors, or represents the invention of a fictional character by the editing processes is a matter now beyond resolution. But in effect the colophon, along with those elements in the editorial framework which name Jeremiah, has created the figure of Jeremiah as the person responsible for the utterance of the words. So many of the speeches and poems are tied in to an identified speaker only by virtue of the framework that the importance of recognizing the contribution of the editors to the creation of the Jeremiah tradition cannot be over-emphasized.

The work of the editors in the creation of the book can be seen in a number of different features. Long stretches of poetry are broken up by prose pieces which allow for a framework attribution of speech, action or occasion to connect with Jeremiah (e.g. 7.1; 11.1; 14.1; 18.1; 21.1, 3; 25.1-7; 26.1; 27.1; 29.1; 30.1-3; 32.1; 33.1; 34.1; 35.1; 36.1-3; 37.1-2; 40.1; 44.1; 45.1; 46.1). Many of these could be removed without affecting what follows. Some of them pose serious problems of interpretation for the exegete, and this suggests that their secondary nature belongs to a different stage of the construction of the book (e.g. 27.1; 28.1; 32.1-5). Repetitions of small units of text, especially in the MT, constitute a series of doublets which necessarily indicates editorial activity. These repeated elements may be part of an editorial scheme to link up certain sections or to draw attention to certain emphases within the larger work, but at this distance from the creation of the Jeremiah tradition it is not possible to explain the phenomenon. The main doublets may be seen in 6.13-15=8.10-12; 11.20=20.12: 16.14-15=23.7-8; 23.5-6=33.14-16; 23.19-20=30.23-24; 30.10-11=46.27-28; 49.19-21=50.44-46.

There are also more complex uses of material which is common to a number of different biblical books: e.g. 25.30 shares elements with Amos 1.2 and Joel 3.16 (MT 4.16); 48.43-46 has links with Isa. 24.17-18b; Num. 21.19, 28; 24.17b; 49.14-16 is very similar to Obad. 1-4. These features of the book demand a more complicated account of the editing of the Jeremiah tradition and suggest a common pool of poems used interchangeably to construct parts of different books (note the citation of Mic. 3.12 in 26.18). The gathering together of discrete elements with a common theme may be seen in the collections assembled in 7.1–8.3 (cultic matters); 14.1–15.4 (drought and war to some extent); 21.11–23.6 (royal house and city); 23.9-40 (the prophets); 27-29 (prophets and Babylon); 30-33 (book of restoration of the fortunes of Israel with prose appendices); 37-38 (Jeremiah and Zedekiah); 40.7–41.18 (Gedaliah's community without Jeremiah); 46-51 (OAN). This dominant feature of the book indicates something of how the editors collected thematic material and presented it as a series of small blocks within the larger structures of Jeremiah. There are also minor scribal indicators which draw attention to technical features of the text; e.g. 'thus far is the judgment on Moab' (48.47); 'thus far are the words of Jeremiah' (51.64).

More complex editorial patterns may be detected in the shaping of the book: the temple sermon in 7.1-15 is repeated to some extent in 26.1-6, but the development of the story in 26.7-24 provides a brilliant beginning to part III and makes connections with the conclusion of that part in 36 (e.g. the presence and absence of prophet and king, social strata etc). 36.1-3 parallels 25.1-7 but is developed significantly in very different ways. Encounters between Jeremiah and Zedekiah (or his delegation) run through the book from 21 to 38, though only 37, 38 are associated together. Datings in the editorial framework link 26.1; 27.1; 28.1; 29.1, and in 26-44 there is, to some extent, a chronological sequence which, omitting 30-31 and ignoring the reverse order of 34, 35, 36, moves from the beginning of Jehoiakim's reign to the collapse of Jerusalem, the humiliation of Gedaliah's community and the retreat to Egypt (spoiled by the placement of 45!).

This general chronological order, fragmented in part III but logical in part IV, is conspicuously absent in part I. In chs. 30-36 there is no slavish devotion to chronology (cf. 21, 24), whereas in 2-20 there is absolutely no chronological information whatever (the only kings named are Josiah in 3.6 and Manasseh in 15.4). This striking difference between 2-20 and 26-45 (with 21-24 reflecting the style of 26-45) must indicate something about distinctive editorial treatments of the two major parts of the book, but what that might be is impossible to determine. It may point to two very different halves of the book having been worked on by separate editorial groups and bound together by an editorial framework with little interest in dating texts chronologically. Such a suggestion is inevitably speculative, but the differences between 2–20 and (21–24) and 26–45 are certainly noteworthy. Guessing editorial policy from the way the text has been edited is an interesting game, but not one which can be pursued successfully by appeals to concrete evidence. The chronological defects of 2–20 are often made good by individual commentators who provide schemes of dating for the different chapters: e.g. Rudolph treats 1–6 as belonging to the time of king Josiah and 7–20 as mainly coming from the time of king Jehoiakim; Holladay confidently dates chapters and portions of chapters to specific dates, events and even weeks in particular years. While there are no textual warrants for such readings of 2–20, the interpretative moves involved are but an extension of the editorial framework employed in 21–45 to complete the unfinished work of the editors who, for reasons beyond our knowing, have left 2–20 incomplete (cf. the equally unfinished titling of the five volumes of psalms in the book of Psalms in terms of the life of David). There are many other features of the editorial framework which contribute to a complex cross-referencing of material in the book of Jeremiah (cf. 25.1-7 with 36.1-3), but these are too complicated to consider here.

Further Reading

Most large-scale commentaries discuss the editions of Jeremiah. The most valuable and detailed discussion of the differences between MT and LXX is to be found in McKane, xv-xli. For the text and critical apparatus of the Hebrew and Greek of Jeremiah:

W. Rudolph (ed.), *Liber Jeremiae* (BHS), 1970

J. Ziegler (ed.), *Ieremias, Baruch, Threni, Epistula Ieremiae*, Septuaginta XV, 1957

Discussion of LXX edition of Jeremiah:

J.G. Janzen, *Studies in the Text of Jeremiah* (Harvard Semitic Monographs 6), 1973.

S. Soderlund, *The Greek Text of Jeremiah: A Revised Hypothesis*, (JSOTS 47), 1985.

E. Tov, 'The Literary History of the Book of Jeremiah in the Light of its Textual History', in J.H. Tigay (ed.), *Empirical Models for Biblical Criticism*, Philadelphia: University of Pennsylvania Press, 1985, 211-37.

A more general consideration of the LXX is E. Tov, *The Text-Critical Use of the Septuagint in Biblical Research* (Jerusalem Biblical Studies 3), Jerusalem: Simor Ltd, 1980. Soderlund's book offers some useful criticisms of recent analyses of the LXX in relation to Jeremiah studies.

On the relative statistics of the variations between the MT and the LXX texts:

Y.-J. Min, 'The Minuses and Pluses of the LXX Translation of Jeremiah as Compared with the Massoretic Text: Their Classification and Possible Origins' (unpublished thesis, Hebrew University, Jerusalem, 1977).

Some access to this thesis is afforded by Soderlund's book.

Comparative translations of the prose sections of MT and LXX:

L. Stulman, *The Other Text of Jeremiah: A Reconstruction of the Hebrew Text Underlying the Greek Version of the Prose Sections of Jeremiah with English Translation*, New York: University Press of America, 1985.

The Targum (Aramaic translation of Hebrew text) of Jeremiah:

R. Hayward, *The Targum of Jeremiah: Translated with a Critical Introduction, Apparatus, and Notes* (The Aramaic Bible 12), Edinburgh: T. & T. Clark, 1987.

On the deuteronomistic edition (see also 'Further Reading' to Chapter 4):

J.P. Hyatt, 'The Deuteronomic Edition of Jeremiah', in *Vanderbilt Studies in the Humanities* I, ed. R.C. Beatty, J.P. Hyatt, & M.K. Spears, Nashville: Vanderbilt University Press, 1951, 71-95 (= Perdue & Kovacs, 247-67).

L. Stulman, *The Prose Sermons of the Book of Jeremiah: A Redescription of the Correspondences with the Deuteronomistic Literature in the Light of Recent Text-critical Research* (SBLDS 83), Atlanta: Scholars Press, 1986.

W. Thiel, *Die deuteronomistische Redaktion von Jeremia 1–25* (WMANT 41, 1973); *idem, Die deuteronomistische Redaktion von Jeremia 26–45* (WMANT 52, 1981), Neukirchen-Vluyn: Neukirchener Verlag.

Chronological readings of the text:

W.L. Holladay, 'A Chronology of Jeremiah's Career', *Jeremiah* 1, 1-10; *idem*, 'A Coherent Chronology of Jeremiah's Early

Career', in Bogaert, 58-73; *idem*, 'The Years of Jeremiah's Preaching', *Interpretation* 37, 1983, 146-59.

W. Rudolph, *Jeremia*, 1.

4

THEORIES OF THE
FORMATION
OF THE BOOK

WHAT DO WE KNOW ABOUT the origins of the books of the
Hebrew Bible? Nothing! How did they come to be written
down in the first place? We do not know! When, why, where and by
whom were they written? No reliable information exists to answer
such basic questions. To every question of this kind the honest
answer is inevitably 'we do not know!' We really do *know* nothing
about the origins and formation of the books in the Hebrew Bible.
This nescience holds good for the book of Jeremiah also. Now
scholars are never satisfied with confessions of ignorance and, in the
absence of firm information, seek to construct theories or develop
analogies from known sources which will illuminate or explain the
data under scrutiny. All such constructions are inevitably theoretical
and hypothetical, but in the absence of factual data to work with they
should not be dismissed as imaginative or as being merely theoretical.
What else could they be? Yet no theory is better than its explanatory
power and, with reference to the Bible, must help to make sense of
the text *as it stands*. Each theory in turn may be replaced by a better
one, i.e. one which provides a more adequate account of the text. Of
the various theories about the formation of the book of Jeremiah the
following may be regarded as the most significant of this century.

For many centuries the traditional views of Jews and Christians
about the authorship of Jeremiah were inevitably of a conventional,
dogmatic or unscholarly nature. They held that the book had been
written by Jeremiah himself or by his companion and secretary
Baruch. The Babylonian Talmud asserts that not only did Jeremiah
write his own book but that he also wrote Kings (*Baba Batra* 15a).
Some modern scholars have advanced similar views (e.g. Friedman),
but generally scholarship in this century has rejected traditional
views for many good reasons (having to do with lack of direct

evidence and internal confusions within the book itself) and has offered a number of alternative theories to account for the existence of the book. Many of the features set out in the previous chapter contribute to the necessity for some such theory to explain the existence and composition of Jeremiah. Thus in modern Jeremiah studies the belief in Jeremiah (or Baruch) as the book's author, though still held by some scholars (e.g. Bright, Holladay, Rudolph), may be assigned a place in the history of the interpretation of the book rather than treated as a contribution to theories about its formation. There is however in much modern writing about Jeremiah a tendency to work with an implicit eyewitness or earwitness theory of its composition which, though never argued for, allows for the attributing sections of the book to the prophet Jeremiah. There is no evidence of a concrete nature to back up this theory. It may be a reasonable viewpoint, but it cannot be corroborated by assuming the truth of the text and *then* arguing from the text for the claim! This would be a circular argument following question-begging procedures and most unscholarly.

The shape of twentieth-century scholarship on the formation of the book of Jeremiah has been moulded by the work of Bernhard Duhm and Sigmund Mowinckel. Duhm's fine 1901 commentary has proved to be seminal (as indeed was his great commentary on the book of Isaiah): he divided the book into poetry and prose and argued that it consists of three parts. These parts consist of 1. the poems of Jeremiah (280 verses), 2. the book of Baruch containing Jeremiah's biography (220 verses), and 3. a further 850 verses supplied by the supplementers of the book. Thus the bulk of the book does not come from Jeremiah but reflects the development of the figure of Jeremiah in a later period in the direction of a presentation of him as a preacher (using prophetic legend and midrashic techniques). The lack of an English translation of his commentary has meant that Duhm's style and many insights into the text have not had the public currency they deserve. However, the division of the book into poetry and prose remains a dominant feature of Jeremiah studies, so Duhm's influence lives on in modern scholarship.

Equally influential (some would say more so) has been Mowinckel's contribution to the understanding of the formative processes behind the book of Jeremiah. In his 1914 work he isolated four sources (A, B, C, D), each with its own redactor (R). Thus the book is the work of various editors (R^ABCD) who put together chs. 1–45, with a later appendix in 46–52, and was completed by R^J. This alphabetic source-equation is to be explained as follows: A stands for the poetry in 1–25 and, according to Mowinckel, indicates the 'very words of Jeremiah' (*ipsissima verba Jeremiae*); B is made up of historical tales which depict the prophet in action (e.g. 19.1-2, 10-11; 19.14–20.6; 26–44); consists of the speeches which do not belong to A or B (e.g. 7.1–8.3; 11.1-14; 18.1-12; 21.1-10; 25.1-11; 32.1-2, 6-16, 24–44; 34; 35; 44.1-14) and which reflect linguistic and theological features similar to the deuteronomistic writings; D is an inserted collection of oracles (30–31), with the addition of 31.29-40; 33. The chronological sequence of these sources is that A is from the sixth–fifth century BCE, B is later than A, from the end of the fifth century (C); D is undatable. In his 1946 book Mowinckel changed his mind about treating these strands as sources and decided that they constituted 'tradition complexes'.

Further refinements in the development of Mowinckel's sources/complexes A, B, C (D has dropped out of use in post-Mowinckel studies) may be found in the work of John Bright, William Holladay, and Helga Weippert, special attention being paid to C (the deutero-nomistic level in the book). This source or tradition-complex is the most controversial aspect of theories of the formation of the book of Jeremiah. There is no agreement among scholars as to whether it represents the actual words of Jeremiah, the gist of what he said, invented words put into his mouth, or a deuteronomistic set of sermons creatively attributed to him (see Chapter 3 above). Here the arguments are often technical and complex, and are dominated by the monographs of Weippert and Thiel. If Thiel has developed Hyatt's work to its logical conclusions, Bright, Holladay and Weippert have taken a very different track in their understanding of what such prose sermons indicate about the growth of the tradition.

Bright sees no essential difference between the B and C strands and believes them to represent 'a single stream of transmission through which Jeremiah's words have been handed down' (1966, 23). Weippert's monograph is a very sharp and useful analysis of the prose speeches in the book. She characterizes them as displaying a specialized prose (*Kunstprosa*) of a highly stylized type peculiar to the book of Jeremiah and attributable to the prophet himself. Her work has certainly demonstrated that there is a style and vocabulary distinctively belonging to the book of Jeremiah, but it does not follow

from this set of features that Jeremiah is their author. Holladay's
work has followed similar lines to Weippert's (he is very much in
agreement with her analysis). He has detected poetic traces behind
some of the prose (thus showing that the development of the
tradition is even more complex than appeared at first to be the case!)
and has linked many of the speeches to specific occasions in the life of
Jeremiah. In his approach to the text he sees it as a code to which the
key is his thesis that these prose sermons are Jeremiah's counter-
proclamations to the septennial readings of the book of Deuteronomy
(cf. Deut. 31.10-13). Beginning in the autumn of 622 on the occasion
when the deuteronomic law was proclaimed publicly for the first
time, Jeremiah made further counter-statements at all subsequent
readings, in the years 615, 608, 601, 594, 587 (we should note that
since according to Holladay the prophet was born in 627 he would
have been twelve years old when he gave his first anti-Deuteronomy
speech!). None of the theories offered about the prose of Jeremiah is
without its problems, and the reader needs to be wary of the
theoretical conclusions which are often attached to acute linguistic
analyses of the data.

In the first volume of his magisterial commentary on Jeremiah
William McKane offers a different and somewhat distinctive
approach to the prose of Jeremiah and the formation of 1–25. He
argues for a 'rolling corpus' notion of the book's development. A
rolling corpus is a body of texts which is built up by the gradual
accretion of further texts generated by an original core of material.
The poetry may generate further poetry and even prose (cf. 3.1-20 for
a complex sequence of poetry and prose elements illustrating
McKane's claim), and the prose may generate more prose. Thus
much of 1–25 can be seen as an intensely convoluted exegetical
development in which bits of text generate others and the book grows
under its own constraints to become a rather untidy and somewhat
haphazard collection of pieces. McKane's analysis has the unusual
virtue of recognizing the untidiness of the biblical text and the
tensions existing between various parts of it. It also offers a fairly
non-technical account of how parts of the book may have arisen in
the first place. A useful exercise for the reader wishing to grasp the
different approaches to the text of Jeremiah would be to compare
McKane and Holladay on the background settings posited for various
passages in 1–25. Understanding the way distinctive presuppositions

and analyses make for very different readings can be instructive. McKane attributes most of the poetry in 1–25 to Jeremiah—an acknowledged assumption, but one that so many commentators and exegetes make. Without some such assumptions the text of Jeremiah will remain a closed book for many readers; but assumptions should always be recognized as such and not allowed subtly to become established facts!

Equally problematic is the location of the producers and production of the text. Palestine, Babylonia, and Egypt are all represented in the book as places where the Judeans survived the fall of Jerusalem and the deprivations of the Babylonian conquest of Palestine. At times the text speaks with a Jerusalem or Judean perspective (e.g. 'this place' in 7.6; 24.5; 'folly in Israel' in 29.23), but the pro-Babylonian attitudes of certain passages (e.g. 24; 29) allow some scholars to argue for a social location of the tradition in Babylon (countered by 42.7-12?). Those who regard Jeremiah as his own author, editor and even publisher (e.g. Holladay, Lundbom) may claim a Palestinian or perhaps an Egyptian location for the book. Others who see in the deuteronomistic sermons the preaching of circles among the exiles in Babylon necessarily posit a Babylonian setting for the tradition (e.g. Nicholson). A different approach to the text which discerns traces of synagogal influence behind the book (e.g. Volz) may place it in Palestine or Babylon. Little in the book can be extrapolated in such a way that it provides good evidence for locating the producers of the Jeremiah tradition. Furthermore, the differences between the first and second editions of the book indicate that its growth and formation were fairly fluid over a long period of time and that, until at least the second century BCE, no *fixed* text existed.

Besides these various theories of the book's origins and formation there is the story in 36 which represents Baruch the scribe (v. 32) as writing at Jeremiah's dictation a scroll (*m^egillat-sēfer*) of his words from the time of Josiah until 605 (36.2; cf. 1.2-3; 25.1-7). This scroll was then read out by Baruch to the people gathered in the temple for a fast (as part of the fast liturgy?). In v. 9 there is a shift of a year between the original writing of the scroll and Baruch's reading of it (LXX reads 'eighth year', i.e. 601). The story is quite complex at this point as v. 8 implies that Baruch had already carried out Jeremiah's instructions by reading the scroll in the temple, whereas v. 9 tells a highly structured story about *three* readings of the scroll and the

outcome of the final reading before the king. Many scholars read ch.
36 as if it were a straightforward historical account not only of what
happened on one particular occasion but as a reliable testimony of
how prophetic books, especially that of Jeremiah, came to be written.
They extrapolate from 36 a paradigm of the transformation of the
spoken word into the written text. How this could be known is a
mystery. 36 cannot be used first to demonstrate how prophetic texts
were written and then as evidence to confirm that 36 is historically
accurate. That is to argue in circles by using 36 as evidence for the
truth claims about 36! The story is a fascinating piece of literature
and one of the finest in the book of Jeremiah, but its historicity
cannot be assumed without serious arguments to support that
contention. Its literariness, its connections with 26 and 25.1-11 (the
summary to part I), and its structural parallels with 2 Kings 22
should warn the reader not to read it simply as an eyewitness account
of what happened in 605/604/601 (those datings should tell against
such simpstic readings of complex texts!).

Baruch appears at a few points in the book apart from 36 (32.12-
13; 43.3, 6; 45.1-2) and has been regarded on the strength of these few
references to have been Jeremiah's companion, secretary, confidant,
and amanuensis. In extra-biblical literature he and Jeremiah appear
as legendary companions (see Chapter 7 below), but the few allusions
to him in the biblical book hardly warrant reading Jeremiah as if
Baruch were behind the creation of the book itself. The few strands
in which he does appear are complex constructions in the tradition
and do not yield a coherent or unified picture of Baruch (cf. Wanke).
Baruch has been identified with the person alluded to on a recently
discovered bulla (a seal for attaching to documents) bearing the
inscription *lbrkyhw bn nryhw hsfr*. This may be translated loosely as
'belonging to Birk\u1ebbyahu (Baruch?) son of Nir\u1ebbyahu the scribe' (such
variations in spelling may be found in Jer. 27–29, though not of
Baruch's name). Now archaeological finds (forgeries apart) are too
open to multiplicity of interpretations for this small seal to be
considered as having anything germane to contribute to Jeremiah
studies. It certainly does not warrant the claim that 'we have the
signature of the recorder—and possibly the author/editor—of eight
books of the Bible' (Friedman, p. 148). The text of Jeremiah will not
yield so easily to the simplicities of bad heremeneutics. According to
29.1; 30.2; 51.60 Jeremiah does his own writing, so the introduction

of a professional scribe in 36 is both unusual and necessitates interpretation. Does 36 incorporate a clue about the takeover of the tradition by the deuteronomists and an insinuation of themselves into the story of Jeremiah? What is the relation between the stories of Jeremiah and Baruch in the Bible and outside it? Apart from 36 Baruch is a very shadowy figure in the book, but he comes into his own in the extra-biblical literature. Perhaps then the few third-person references to Baruch are the beginnings of the long story of Jeremiah and Baruch which forms an important part of the pseudepigraphal literature and represents a common theme of literary concerns characteristic of the age of pseudepigraphy.

In the story set out in 36 the king burns (or has burned) the scrolls, a few columns at a time, thus necessitating its rewriting. In the second scroll produced by Jeremiah and Baruch a longer document comes into existence due to the addition of further words to it (v. 32). Those scholars who read 36 in a literal fashion include some who have analyzed the text of Jeremiah in relation to the two scrolls. Thus Holladay offers an identification of the contents of the two scrolls as they now appear in 1–20. The only clue to what words the original scroll may have contained is given in 36.29 and concerns the invasion of the land by the king of Babylon. A few pieces in 2–20 may be relevant to that summary, but the bulk of the material *now* contained in 2–20 does not belong to such a theme and can hardly be regarded as the meaning of the vague phrase 'and also many words *like them*' (36.32). The interpretative moves of scholars vis-à-vis the two scrolls of 36 illustrate many of the problems of interpreting Jeremiah and underline the depth of our ignorance about the formation of the book.

One element in the composition of the book which seems to command the assent of most scholars is the view that the poems in 2–20 contain the genuine words of Jeremiah. Even McKane works with this assumption. It shows the continued influence of Duhm and is based on the belief that the prophets were fundamentally poets. It is a hypothesis worth entertaining, though there is no hard evidence to support it (except the circular argument entailed in the claim). *If* anything of the 'historical' Jeremiah (a construct of the edited text?) is to be found in the book it may well be that it is to be found in the poetry of 2–20 (also in the poetry of 30–31, 46–51?). Yet the claim that this poetry represents Jeremiah's original utterances is itself a question-begging assumption. The figure of Jeremiah is derived from the editorial framework and the prose narratives and *not* from the poetry! It is also the nature of this kind of poetry that it is anonymous and so requires a framework of a prosaic kind to provide it with a definite attribution (see the references in Carroll, 46-49). It may be inevitable and reasonable that scholars should make some assumptions about the texts they read, but such assumptions only have the status of hypotheses: they do not constitute evidence or knowledge.

Admissions of ignorance here would help to defuse the romanticism of many writers on the book of Jeremiah. Scholarship is a bad place for romanticism! Yet theories are inevitable because it is easier to work with some hypothetical account of formation and origins against which to read the text than to acknowledge ignorance and read the text without a theory of authorship (as Carroll's commentary does). Biblical books do not contain colophons indicating authorship (as some Babylonian cuneiform writings do), but appear to concentrate on the collection of sayings and narratives attributed to an original figure and set in a definite period (e.g. 1.1-3). The text is then expected to be read against such a background, though it does not follow that such a stage direction was an integral part of the text in the first place. Of all the current theories about the formation of the book of Jeremiah, McKane's thesis of its piecemeal growth seems to me to be the most reasonable for 1-25 and also to be an accurate description of certain features of a rather untidy book.

Further Reading

The arguments of Duhm and Mowinckel are to be found in:

Duhm, *Das Buch Jeremia*, XI-XXII.

Mowinckel, *Zur Komposition des Buches Jeremia*, Oslo: Jacob Dybwad, 1914; *idem*, *Prophecy and Tradition: The Prophetic Books in the Light of the Study of the Growth and History of the Tradition*, Oslo: Jacob Dybwad, 1946.

On the treatment of the prose from a non-deuteronomistic perspective:

J. Bright, 'The Date of the Prose Sermons of Jeremiah', *JBL* 70, 1951, 15-35 (= Perdue & Kovacs, 193-212); *idem*, 'The Prophetic Reminiscence: Its Place and Function in the Book of Jeremiah', in *Biblical Essays*, Proceedings of the Ninth Meeting of 'Die Ou-Testamentische Werkgemeenskap in Suid-Afrika', 1966, 11-30.

W.L. Holladay, 'Prototype and Copies: A New Approach to the
Poetry-Prose Problem in the Book of Jeremiah', *JBL* 79,
1960, 351-67 ; *idem* 'A Fresh Look at "Source B" and
"Source C" in Jeremiah', *VT* 25, 1975, 394-412 (=
Perdue & Kovacs, 213-28).

H. Weippert, *Die Prosareden des Jeremiabuches*, BZAW 132,
1973.

The respective merits of the approaches of Weippert and Thiel (*Die
deuteronomistische Redaktion von Jeremia 1-25/26-45*) are discussed by W.
McKane, 'Relations Between Poetry and Prose in the Book of Jeremiah with
Special Reference to Jeremiah III 6-11 and XII 14-17', *Congress Volume*:
Vienna 1980 (SVT 32), 1981, 220-37 (= Perdue & Kovacs, 269-84); also in
his *Jeremiah* I, xli-xlvii.

On the social location of Jeremiah the arguments are necessarily inferential:
the logic of J.R. Lundbom, *Jeremiah: A Study in Ancient Hebrew Rhetoric*
(SBLDS 18), Missoula, 1975, which makes Jeremiah and, in particular,
Baruch the arrangers of their own work would place them and therefore the
book in preexilic Jerusalem! E.W. Nicholson, *Preaching to the Exiles: A
Study of the Prose Tradition in the Book of Jeremiah*, Oxford: Blackwell,
1970, attributes the prose sections to preaching circles in Babylon. For
connections between Jeremiah and the synagogue see E. Janssen, *Juda in der
Exilszeit: Ein Beitrag zur Frage der Entstehung des Judentums* (FRLANT
69), 1956, 105-15; cf. Smith, *Palestinian Parties*, 77-78. K.-F. Pohlmann,
*Studien zum Jeremiabuch: Ein Beitrag zur Frage nach der Entstehung des
Jeremiabuches* (FRLANT 118), 1978, 183-97, locates 21; 24; 37-44 in the
fourth century as an 'exile-orientated redaction' of the book of Jeremiah.

On 36 and theories about the two scrolls:

Holladay, *The Architecture of Jeremiah 1-20*, Lewisburg: Bucknell
University Press, 1976; *idem*, 'The Identification of the
Two Scrolls of Jeremiah', *VT* 30, 1980, 452-67.

C. Rietzschel, *Das Problem der Urrolle: Ein Beitrag zur Redaktionsgeschichte des Jeremiabuches*, Gütersloh: Gütersloher
Verlagshaus Gerd Mohn, 1966.

G. Wanke, *Untersuchungen zur sogenannten Baruchschrift* (BZAW
122), 1971, argues for three very different strands of
material on Baruch.

The material remains unearthed by archaeologists which have yielded the
name of Baruch (or a similar form), are discussed in N. Avigad, 'Baruch the
Scribe and Jerahmeel the King's Son', *Israel Exploration Journal* 28, 1978,

52-56; *idem, Hebrew bullae from the time of Jeremiah: Remnants of a burnt archive*, Israel Exploration Society, Jerusalem, 1986, 28-29, 128-30, On Baruch the writer of various biblical books see R.E. Friedman, *Who Wrote the Bible?*, New York: Summit Books, 1987, 146-49.

Further discussion of the theories of formation may be found in any competent *OT Introduction* or large-scale commentary; see also Carroll, *Jeremiah*, 38-50; L.G. Perdue, 'Jeremiah in Modern Research: Approaches and Issues', in Perdue & Kovacs, 14-22.

5

CYCLES OF
POETRY
AND PROSE

T HE DISTINCTION BETWEEN POETRY and prose in the book of Jeremiah has been an important feature of Jeremiah studies this century (cf. Duhm, McKane), though recent studies have raised interesting difficulties about the definition of biblical poetry. Some writers on Jeremiah have argued for a greater degree of poetry in the book than has often been thought to be the case (e.g. Condamin, Holladay). A lengthy theoretical discussion about the nature of poetry in the Bible and the extent to which Jeremiah is poetry or prose cannot be undertaken here, but the wise reader may reflect on the subject after a careful reading of 36 (prose) and 51 (mostly poetry). Both styles are to be found throughout Jeremiah, though there is a preponderance of poetry in 2-25 with a corresponding weighting of prose in 26-51. Often the two styles are intermingled in a single thematic cycle (e.g. 14.1-15.4; 21.11-23.6; 30.1-31.40), and it is very difficult to isolate a cycle of poetry which does not contain some prose. On the other hand, there are cycles of prose which appear to have no poetic elements in them (e.g. 27-29; 39-44), as well as many individual narratives. In order to break up the bulk of material in the book of Jeremiah into more convenient sections for treatment here I shall devote a chapter to the poetry cycles and another one to the narratives. This division of labour is purely one of convenience and little else follows from it. No cycle of poetry can be given a thematic unity without its becoming obvious to the intelligent reader that the descriptive category is only an extrapolation from *part* of the cycle and *not* an accurate descriptive account of everything in the cycle (e.g. the 'foe from the north' theme of 4.5-6.26 is only derived from a few of the poems in 4-6 and does not represent them all).

In part I (2.1–25.14) there are six cycles of poetry and prose, with 25.1-14 functioning as an epilogue. A prologue to this part appears in 1, and this consists mainly of prose elements with a poem in vv. 4-10. There are certain structural links between this prologue and the epilogue: for example, the twenty-three years of 1.2-3 (by calculation from Josiah's thirteenth year, i.e. 627, to the fourth year of Jehoiakim, i.e. 605), which are made explicit in 25.3, but are only implicit in 1.3 (though both texts share Josiah's thirteenth year); the coming of the divine word to Jeremiah (1.2, 4, 11, 13; 25.1, 3); the tribes of the north (1.15; 25.9). The important poem in 1.4-10 declares at the outset of the book the validation of the speaker as a prophet to the nations, an authorization confirmed by the visions of vv. 11-14. Additional prose material in 1.15-19 develops the second vision and interprets it as a statement *against* the kings (!) of Judah and the people. There are links between 1.17-19 and 6.27-30; 15.20-21.

First cycle (2–6)
This cycle is made up of two main parts with some thematic unity: 2.5–4.4 are a lengthy haranguing of the community for cultic offences and 4.5–6.30 are a collection of discrete poems, in some of which a 'foe from the north' motif can be discerned (e.g. 4.5-8; 6.1-5, 22-26). The cycle has a prologue in 2.1-3, a mixture of prose introduction and a poem (cf. the youth motif in 1.6; 2.2). The haranguing of the community for religious apostasy in the past and present is made up of a series of poems, with some prose commentary in 3.6-11, 15-18, 24-25. A feature of this first cycle is the number of sexual metaphors which are used to condemn the religious practices of the people (e.g. 2.20, 23-24; 3.1, 3, 6-9, 20, 23; 4.30; 5.7-8). Some of these metaphors are quite obscene, but such obscenities are a feature of books such as Jeremiah and Ezekiel.

Liturgical elements have been detected in 2.4–4.4, and these may indicate a preaching or proto-synagogal setting for the original poems (now decontextualized by removal from worshipping origins and located in a book). Behind the harangues may be an ideology of correct belief and worship reflecting the propaganda of a 'Yahweh-alone' cult directed against the more inclusive worship of earlier Jerusalem cults. The poems about the enemy from the north share echoes with the OAN of 50–51 (cf. 6.22-24 with 50.41-43), and in the

MT these collections, 4-6 and 50-51, provide a symmetry to the book lacking in the earlier edition represented by the LXX. The irony of the similarities should be noted, though it cannot be shown which came first (most scholars would make 4-6 the more original). Throughout 4-6 the devastated city speaks under the guise of a violated woman or distraught mother (e.g. 4.19-21, 30-31; in Hebrew the gender of cities is feminine, hence the personification of Jerusalem as a woman). Other poems stress the incorrigibility of the people (4.22; 5.1-5, 11, 21, 25; 6.6-7, 10, 13-15, 17) and contribute towards the making of a theodicy (a theological justification of the deity in the face of evil experienced in the world) which would account for the destruction of Jerusalem.

Second cycle (8-10)
The rest of the cycles are introduced by the editorial framework phrase 'the word of Yahweh which came to Jeremiah' (with minor variations; 2.1 assumes 1.1-3) and consist of mixtures of prose and poetry. 7.1-8.3 is a lengthy collection of mainly prose pieces (poetic elements appear in 7.28-29) held together by the thematic motif of cultic practices and attitudes. All the practices associated with temple and sacrifice are condemned, and the section provides some parallels with the poetic haranguing of the community in 2.4-4.4. Usually regarded as deuteronomistic in language, thought and style, these attacks on cultic behaviour allow an association of religion and the destruction of Jerusalem to condemn those who might have wished to be identified with the cultic life of the community (of the past?). The temple sermons of 7.5-7, 8-15 link the destruction of the temple to the ethics of the people, and the 'amendment of life' motif in 7.5-7 is reproduced in 26.2-6. The family religion of 7.17-19 is taken up in a very different context in 44.15-19, 24-28. 7.16 is repeated in 11.14 (cf. 14.11). The polemic against sacrifice in 7.21-26 has echoes in 6.20, and the metaphor used in 7.25 (i.e. the early rising god) appears in 7.13; 11.7; 25.4; 26.5; 29.19; 32.33; 35.14, 15; 44.4 with varying uses. The fire-cult at Topheth in 7.31-33 is also one of the subjects of 19.3-13. 7.34 is reversed in 33.10-11. The poems in 8.4-9.11 are a mixture of denunciations of the community for corruption and incorrigibility and laments for the devastation of Jerusalem. Two laments and some prose reflections on wisdom constitute 9.12-26. 10.1-16 is a unique assemblage of poems warning

Israel against the religion of the nations (after 2–4!). In terms of polemic against the gods of the nations and a hymn of Yahweh's incomparability (10.12-16 = 51.15-19). The two editions differ considerably in 10.4-11, though both versions are coherent and cogent. Most peculiar is the fact that v. 11 is in Aramaic rather than Hebrew! It appears to be some sort of magical incantation directed against cult opponents (Duhm), though its content is banal. Everything in the poem runs counter to the tenor and sense of 2–20. The cycle ends with a few poetic elements: an oracle against the city (vv. 17-18), a lament by the city-community (vv. 19-20), with a coda criticizing the leadership (v. 21; cf. 2.8), a fragment of the enemy from the north motif (v. 22), and a concluding communal prayer for divine discipline of the speaker and destruction of the nations (vv. 23-25).

Third cycle (11–13)

A lengthy prose piece presents Jeremiah as a preacher of the convenant in 11.1-13; this covenant is preached in the cities of Judah and in the streets of Jerusalem and its rejection explains why Jerusalem has been destroyed. Many commentators relate this prose sermon to the deuteronomistic reform movement and read it as a deuteronomistic presentation of Jeremiah as an active participant in the reforms of Josiah. Too many interpretative problems are connected with this reading to be discussed here. 11.15-17 could be poetry or prose and the verses are not easily interpreted: perhaps an ironic attack on the cult is behind its present state. A further poetic fragment comparing the people ('my beloved'?) to a green olive tree appears in v. 16 and is linked to the preceding attack on idolatrous practices (1–13) by v. 17. Another poem about the destruction of a tree appears in vv. 18-19, with a prayer for revenge (v. 20 = 20.12). This poem now has attached to it a prose commentary about a plot by the men of Anathoth. It is obscure in the extreme. A lament about the prosperity of the wicked (12.1-4) is followed by two poetic fragments in 12.5, 6 (see below for interpretation). A poem in 12.7-13 laments the destruction of the nation and its temple and is balanced by a warning to the nations about learning the ways of Judah (v. 16 reverses 10.2 by insisting on the nations' conformity to Judean religion). 13.1-7 is a prose narrative of a kind found throughout the book (see Chapter 6 below) which involves the speaker in a symbolic or magical action; to it is added an interpretation of the meaning of this action (vv. 8-11). A proverb with explanatory expansion follows in vv. 12-14 and the cycle ends with a series of poems (vv. 15-27) on different subjects: a warning and a lament (vv. 15-17), a brief oracle to the king and his mother (vv. 18-19; a unique reference to such in chs. 2-20), and various poems condemning the community under the figure of a woman (vv. 20-27, with obscene elements in vv. 21, 26-27).

Fourth cycle (14-17)
The editorial framework provides a prose verse with which to introduce a cycle of poems and prose under the general heading 'concerning the drought' (14.1; 14.2-15.4). Apart from 14.2-6 there is little in this cycle which can specifically be tied to the drought motif: thus 14.1 is more a title to vv. 2-6 than to the whole cycle. The dominant form is that of the lament (vv. 7-9, 17-19), with various oracular responses (vv. 10, 11-12, 14, 15-16; 15.1, 2-4) and a communal acknowledgment of guilt (vv. 20-22). The interweaving of so many different strands may suggest a liturgical pattern behind the present text, but so little is known about the production of the book of Jeremiah that it is always easier to posit a liturgy then to prove one. A lament follows the cycle and is made oracular by the phrases 'says Yahweh' (15.5-9; cf. vv. 6, 9), as if Yahweh were both slayer of the community and its chief mourner. A badly preserved piece of text appears in 15.10-14 (vv. 13-14 may be a variant of 17.3-4) and there are considerable differences between the two editions of v. 11. A lament follows in vv. 15-18 in which the speaker appeals to Yahweh for vengeance and complains about incurable pain. An oracular response is added to this lament in which the one addressed is supported by the deity against the people. The cycle continues with a series of prose pieces (16.1-4, 5-9, 10-13, 14-15[=23.7-8], 16-18, 21) and a brief poem (16.19-20). Central to these pieces is the notion of the divine destruction of the nation because of its idolatrous practices. 17.1-4 spells out this destruction and describes the idolatrous ways of the people in graphic metaphors. A series of poems using wisdom motifs contrasts the difference between those who are cursed and those who are blessed (17.5-8), with further poems stressing the fate of those who forsake Yahweh (17.9-13; each element here is essentially a working out of the contrasts of vv. 5-8).

A prayer for healing follows (vv. 14-18) and the cycle ends with a lengthy prose piece on sabbath regulations.

Fifth cycle (18-20)

The initial prose presents Jeremiah as going down (from the temple?) to the potter's house; his observations of the potter's habits give rise to post-deuteronomistic style reflections on the nature of national turnings (18.1-12). A graphic poem condemns the Israelite nation for idolatry (vv. 13-17). A lament in vv. 19-23 appealing to Yahweh for vengeance against the families of the speaker's tormentors is turned into a response of Jeremiah's by a prose heading in v. 18. Two lengthy pieces of prose develop the motifs of the potter and the temple in 19.1-20.6. These are very complicated pieces, and 19.1-13 is a very good example of the complex processes whereby strands of tradition are welded together in the book of Jeremiah. A symbolic action relating to buying and breaking a ceramic flask is mixed with sermons of a deuteronomistic style against idolatrous practices in Jerusalem, and a polemic against the fire-cult at Topheth outside the city. In 19.14-20.6 when Jeremiah returns to the temple (from where he set out in 18.1?) he is beaten up by Pashhur the priest (20.1-2) and, after a night in the stocks, denounces Pashhur by means of a name-changing oracle (20.3-6). A lament (vv. 7-10), a hymn of confidence (vv. 11-13; v. 12=11.20), and a self-cursing or conventional response to bad news ends the cycle (vv. 14-18; cf. Job 3).

The laments in 11-20

The three cycles of material in 11-20 cannot be said to have any obvious unifying factor: prose is followed by poetry, and the two alternate throughout the blocks of text using a variety of motif and subject matter. Sermons, symbolic actions, reflections, and laments seem to be the dominant features of the cycles. However, a number of the laments have been singled out for special scrutiny and, in recent Jeremiah studies, these laments have been given a particularistic interpretation. They are to be found in 11.18-20 (with vv. 21-23); 12.1-6; 15.10-21; 17.14-18; 18.18-23; 20.7-18 and are often referred to as 'the *confessions* of Jeremiah'. That is, they are read as autobiographical utterances of the prophet Jeremiah and treated as representations of his innermost thoughts and prayers. They are not, however, gathered into one place or given any editorial connections with Jeremiah's speaking, though in 11.21-23 and 18.18 the placement of these statements suggests some connection between the laments and the life of Jeremiah. The most natural way to read them would be to treat them as laments protesting the suffering of the righteous at the hands of the wicked and, in the context of the book of Jeremiah with its denunciations of the people in a time of mass destruction caused by invasion, to relate these protestations to an attempt to differentiate between the wicked and the righteous in that time. Unfortunately there are few texts in the book of Jeremiah which yield to an obvious reading of the text's surface meaning, and there are no more highly disputed pieces in Jeremiah than these laments. Hence any account of the laments must be a highly complex piece of interpretative argument, and a wide diversity of possible meanings of the poems must be allowed for.

Many of the poems in 2–20 blame the whole nation for the invasion and defeat of 597/587 by the Babylonians; not one person is excused or recognized as being less than evil (e.g. 5.1-5; 6.13; 8.4-7; 9.2-6, 8; 14.10; 15.6; 18.15). When therefore we encounter some poems which speak on behalf of the righteous against the persecution of the wicked (e.g. 12.1-4; 15.15, 21; 17.18; 18.19-23; 20.11-12 [cf. 11.20]), it is certainly worth viewing these laments as another stage in the development of the tradition: a protest on behalf of the innocent and the righteous who seek divine vindication through their prayers and laments. This reasonable interpretation of what are, by any account and especially in view of the spread of them throughout 11–20, very difficult poems to interpret posits a very different background for them from the theodicy implicit in the poems which blame everybody in the community. We must seek the origins of these laments in circles which, like the producers of the laments in the Psalms, recognized a polarity of righteous and wicked within the one community. Notions of healing and vindication have their setting here and not in any theodicy seeking to explain why city and community were wiped out by the destruction of Jerusalem. The defeat of Judah and Jerusalem by the Babylonians in 587 vindicated nobody! Good and bad (biblical righteous and wicked), rich and poor, just and unjust, men and women, priest and peasant were all swept away in the burning wrath released by the Babylonians. Those who survived famine, pestilence, invasion and execution succumbed to deportation (including Jeremiah and whatever friends he may have had). No healing or vindication was to be found in the aftermath of 587. So the poems which seek vindication on behalf of the righteous against the wicked must be read against a very different backdrop from the fall of Jerusalem.

Whatever the virtues of this reading of the laments in 11–20 it must be acknowledged that the majority of commentators and writers on Jeremiah prefer the 'confessions' approach and read the laments as self-referring statements of the prophet Jeremiah. There are exceptions to this reading (e.g. Reventlow's sophisticated interpretation of the utterances as spoken by Jeremiah in his role of cult prophet and spokesman for the community), but the overwhelming majority of scholars accede to the traditional interpretation of Jeremiah as a speaker of laments (hence the traditional view of Jeremiah as the author of the book of Lamentations; cf. 2 Chron. 35.25). This approach to the laments incorporates readings of the poems as expressions of heartfelt pain and spiritual struggle as well as statements of a mystical nature and examples of the prophet's prayer life. It maximizes a whole range of applicatory understandings of the text which make the perfectly adequate righteous-versus-wicked controversy, so characteristic of biblical pietism, approach appear reductionist in comparison! It also permits very complex coded readings of the texts in which the biblical writers take on the sophistication of twentieth-century writers and produce intricately structured cross-referencing texts of a scholastic nature (cf. Diamond, Polk). In some of these readings Jeremiah utters his laments as evidence of his frustration and pain at the opposition of the 'false' prophets against him (e.g. Holladay, Diamond). Hints of this interpretation may be detected in 11.21 (*not* prophetic opposition but familial!); 14.13-15 (not part of the personal laments at all!); 18.18 (the prophets are mentioned but then so are the priests and the wise men!); 20.1-6 (Pashhur only becomes a prophet by virtue of 20.6 but is otherwise a priest).

It really is difficult to read the laments in a natural context of opposition from the prophets, though many exegetes would happily understand 15.16 and 17.15 as evidence of the prophetic status of the speaker. Capable of other interpretations, these statements hardly justify the *prophetic* status of the wicked/persecutors spoken against. Space does not permit a serious consideration of all the complex and complicated elements germane to this discussion, but I would stress here the fact that this is perhaps the most difficult and, certainly, the most fiercely contested area of interpretation in the study of Jeremiah, and no one viewpoint can be regarded as holding the field. Even biblical scholarship does not operate with a statistical notion of truth, so deference is not necessarily due to the compact majority! Here are pitfalls and problems.

Sixth cycle (21–24)
An appendix consisting of two prose pieces and two cycles of poetry and prose separates part I from its summary in 25.1-14. This appendix is more characteristic of the material in parts III and IV than of that in part I (e.g., the two prose pieces are given specific time settings, whereas no prose in I has such information). Chronological order is not important because 21 is set some ten years *after* 24 (i.e. 587 and 597 ostensibly). 21.1-10 consists of three sections dealing with Zedekiah's delegation to Jeremiah (cf. 37.3-10) in which the annihilation of city and inhabitants is stressed (but with significant variations). 21.11-23.6 constitutes a cycle of poetry and prose about the 'house of the king of Judah' (title in 21.11) and an unnamed city (21.13; 22.6-8, 20-23), presumably now intended to be Jerusalem. The subject matter of the poems, with the exception of 22.28-30, is indefinite, and prose elements provide very necessary interpretations related to the royal house (e.g. 22.11-12, 18a). A very general deuteronomistic piece in 22.1-5 ties the security of the city/palace/ temple ('house' in vv. 1, 4, 5; 'gates' in vv. 2, 4 are ambiguous; cf. 17.19-27) into the ethical behaviour of the royal house (cf. the temple sermon in 7.5-7). Opinions differ on whether 22.24-30 is prose or poetry (RSV treats vv. 24-27 as prose and vv. 28-30 as poetry), and the verses provide a good example of how difficult it can be to differentiate between the two at times.

A prose piece in 23.1-4 (some read this as poetry) condemns the leadership of the community and anticipates new, effective leaders in the future. The cycle ends with two verses (23.5-6) (again the poetry-prose question is disputed) which either refer to king Zedekiah (a wordplay on ṣdq, 'righteous') or look forward to a new king who will guarantee the security of the nation in the future (=33.14-16). 23.7-8 is an independent oracle (=16.14-15) about the future restoration of the diaspora (a technical term for the dispersion of the Jews after the fall of Jerusalem); in the LXX it is placed at the end of 23.40. A cycle of poems and prose pieces under the title 'concerning the prophets' follows on immediately after the royal cycle (thus linking the institutions of kingship and prophecy as root causes of the destruction of Jerusalem?). The speaker is shattered by what is happening throughout the land (vv. 9-10), but the prophets are only isolated as the cause of evil from v. 13 onwards. The godlessness of the age is blamed on the prophets (vv. 14-15), who are accused of not being sent by Yahweh. Their techniques are all wrong (vv. 25-32) and a complex wordplay on the Hebrew word for 'burden' (*maśśā*) concludes the section (vv. 33-40). The cycle concludes with a vision in 24 (see 1.11-14; 38.21-23 for the few other visions in the book; though some exegetes treat 4.23-26; 13.1-7; 25.15-17 also as visions). This vision of two baskets of figs set down in front of the temple (after a complex dating notice in v. 1) gives rise to a complicated oracular explanation which identifies the basket of figs with the exiles of 597 and the basket of rotten figs with Zedekiah's community which remained in Jerusalem after 597 (cf. 29.16-19). The blatant biases of this vision suggest a propaganda role in the tradition for the account, which may have favoured pro-Babylonian community parties in the reconstruction of the city in the Persian period. 24 shares a certain logic with 21.1-7.

Restoration of the fortunes cycle (30–33)
If the first edition were followed the OAN would be dealt with here, but in the second edition that cycle of poems does not appear until 46-51, so the next cycle is the poetry in 30.5-31.22 with various additions in 31.23-33.26. All of this material is held together by the motif 'the restoration of the fortunes' (30.3, 18; 31.23; 32.44; 33.7, 11, 26; cf. 29.14; 48.47; 49.6, 39; the Hebrew phrase may be a wordplay on *šûb* 'turn, return, restore, turn away') and the overwhelming impression made by the four chapters is that of positive rebuilding of community, city and land. A few minor exceptions to this impression may be noted in 30.5-7, 12-15, 23-24 (=23.19-20); 31.30; 32.23-35. The cycle of poems in 30.5-31.22 is introduced by prose elements from the editorial framework (30.1-3, 4) which represent the cycle as a book written by Jeremiah (cf. the letter of 29.4-7 and the book of 51.59-64). Some scholars understand this book of consolation to have been the work of the young Jeremiah when he was eagerly preaching the restoration of northern Israel in the days of Josiah (e.g. Rudolph).

But nothing in 30–31 is datable, so this is by no means a necessary reading of the cycle. Its tenor is much more in keeping with the poems in Isa. 40–55 than with anything in Jer. 2–20, and in 31.2-14 there is a very strong arcadian sense (rather than utopian outlook). The poems are pastoral in tone and positive in expectation, but there is nothing which could date them other than the implicit references to the destroyed Jerusalem (in 30.18-21 the city is not named as it is in 31.6, 12; LXX does not read 'Zion' in 30.17). Destruction of cities and deportations of people are so common an experience for Israel and Judah in the Bible that it is arguable to place these poems anywhere in the history of the two nations, though on balance a postexilic date looks most likely for the completed cycle with its additions and appendices (e.g. 31.23-24, 38-40; 32.42-44; 33.10-11, 12-13, 19-22).

The spirit of the poems in 31.2-14 is so contrary to much of the rest of the book that they are a joy to read. 31.31-34, an addition about a new covenant in the future, has attracted a great deal of attention from Christian theologians due to its use in the New Testament (e.g. Heb. 8.8-13; 10.15-17), though that development of its application really tells us nothing about its meaning in the context of 30–31. In 31.23-40 and 33.13 there is a good deal of reversing of motifs and sayings which once characterized the community's life but which in the future will be transformed. The restoration of the fortunes is the reversal of all the bad luck of the past (for 32 see Chapter 6 below). Most of the prose in this cycle appears in the editorial framework (30.1-3, 4; 31.1) or in the additions to 30.5–31.22 (e.g. 31.23-26, 27-30, 31-34, 38-40; 32; 33).

Oracles against the nations cycle (46–51)
The final cycle of poetry and prose is that of the oracles against the nations. All other cycles are of prose and narrative and have been consigned to the next chapter. The OAN constitute part II of the book of Jeremiah and represent one of the most distinctive differences between the two editions of Jeremiah. In the other two large traditions, Isaiah and Ezekiel, they appear in the middle of the collections (e.g. Isa. 13–23; Ezek. 25–32), as they do in the LXX of Jeremiah. Only in the MT of Jeremiah are they at the end of the book and separated from the listing of the nations (25.19-26) after the summary of part I in 25.1-14. Apart from the prose of 25.15-29 and

the editorial framework of 46.1, 2; 47.1; 48.1; 49.1, 6, 28, 34; 50.1, the bulk of the OAN is poetry (prose sections can be found among the larger groups of OAN, e.g. 48-51). The editors have clearly attributed these poems to Jeremiah the prophet, but it is very difficult to reconcile such an attribution with other features of the whole Jeremiah tradition (contrast, for example, the attitudes of Jeremiah to Babylon in 27-29 and 50-51!). Strong tensions are to be found between the OAN and much of the material associated with Jeremiah. Commentators disagree about the precise relationship of Jeremiah to the OAN, even though 1.5 designates him a 'prophet to the nations', and it is impossible to be dogmatic about how much, if any at all, of the OAN should be attributed to Jeremiah. The MT placement of the OAN at the end of the book allows the work to be enclosed between two statements of Jeremiah's status as a prophet to the nations (1.5, 10; 51.59-64).

As a genre the OAN are to be found in many prophetic collections, apart from the three major ones of Isaiah, Jeremiah, Ezekiel (e.g. Amos 1.3-2.3; Obadiah; Nahum; Zephaniah 2; Zech. 9.1-8; 11.1-3), but their origins and functions in ancient Israel are unknown. According to 28.8 prophets were expected to prophesy 'war, famine, and pestilence *against* many countries and great kingdoms', but the precise nature of this activity is not known to us. Perhaps it was part of the prophetic contribution to nationalistic fervour and chauvinistic activity during times of war against the ancient enemies. The cult and court prophets (e.g. 1 Kgs 22.5-12) may have been employed in rituals of bad luck against and cursings of the enemy, and the OAN may have been the oracles used to accompany such magical activities (cf. the ritual preparations of Balaam and his oracles in the matter of Moab versus Israel in Num. 22.36-24.25). As part of the king's policy of war, prophets may have had a serious contribution to make in generating the proper attitudes among the people and attempting to influence the outcome by their words and rituals. Whatever the theory behind the practice, be it popular xenophobia, support of royal policy, or cult rituals of a magical nature, the presence of the OAN in the various prophetic collections requires some such background explanation.

Again there is no agreement among scholars as to what may be the implications of finding so many OAN in the so-called canonical prophets. If their origins lay in jingoistic rituals of the national cult expressing divine protection of Judah and devastation of the enemy, their presence in traditions quite hostile to such partisan ideals is problematic. It is not necessary to insist that the speakers associated with the various prophetic traditions were themselves also the producers of OAN—no evidence exists either way on this point. The prophetic books appear to have acquired a great deal of disparate material in their transformations into written documents, and there is no good reason for assuming that everything in a book must be attributed directly to the figure named in 1.1 of that book. Scholars who prefer to attribute the *maximal amount of material possible* to the named prophet of each tradition adjust the function, scope and meaning of the OAN to fit in with the presuppositions associated with that prophet so that the problem is resolved in favour of a traditionalist view of the literature. From originally being a war oracle the OAN became the means whereby the prophets tried to influence royal policy and were further transformed by changing circumstances (cf. Christensen). Whatever view is taken of the OAN nothing should be allowed to minimize the complexities involved in understanding these elements as they stand in 46–51 or the problems of relating them to the Jeremiah of other parts of the tradition.

The two editions of Jeremiah not only have different placements of the OAN; they also have a different order of the nations in their lists.

LXX	MT
Elam	Egypt
Egypt	Philistia
Babylon	Moab
Philistia	Ammon
Edom	Edom
Ammon	Damascus
Kedar	Kedar
Damascus	Elam
Moab	Babylon

Little can be said to follow from these differences of listing, though the MT order is *closer* to the listing of the nations in 25.19-26 than is the LXX. MT may represent an attempt to make the order conform to 25.19-26, and that may reflect a secondary development of the tradition. The complex of material in 25.15-38 (LXX 32) is divorced from the OAN in the MT, but appears at the end of the OAN in the

LXX. The listing in 25.19-26 is an expanded one which overlaps with that of 46-51, but each list has names which do not appear on the other.

Some of the best poetry in the book of Jeremiah is to be found in the OAN (e.g. 46.3-12, 14-24; 48.1-10; 50.35-38a; 51.20-23) as well as some of the most difficult. The OAN of Jeremiah also share links with the OAN of Isaiah, Amos, and Obadiah, and this common pattern of motifs and verses militates against an easy ascription of authorship in any of the traditions. The collections against Moab (48) and Babylon (50-51) are the largest. No one theme dominates the OAN, except perhaps the conviction that Yahweh is against all the nations (more pointedly stated in 25.29). At times the reason for this divine opposition is given as hubris on the part of a nation (e.g. 48.26-30, 42), at other times the treatment of Israel affords grounds for Yahweh's destruction of the nations (e.g. 48.27; 50.6-7, 17-20, 28, 33-34; 51.5, 24, 34-37, 49-51). The sense of outrage directed against the depredations of Babylon which appears throughout 50-51 makes this set of OAN a very good foil to the attitude expressed towards Babylon in 27-29, and raises most interesting questions about the ambivalences shown towards Babylon in the book of Jeremiah. Different communities, times and settings may help to ease those ambivalent attitudes by locating 27-29 and 50-51 in distinctive areas and periods, but some explanation is required to account for the contradictory views of Babylon contained in the one book. Ironically Babylon's defeat by the Persians turned out to be nothing like that anticipated or described in 50-51! Perhaps that gap between reality and rhetoric (or celebration) should warn us to read these OAN as more a matter of emotion and gesture than as historical description or expression of political tactics.

Further Reading

Stress on the poetry of Jeremiah is characteristic of the commentaries of Condamin and Thompson. The nature of Hebrew poetry is most usefully introduced by W.G.E. Watson, *Classical Hebrew Poetry: A Guide to its Techniques* (JSOTS 26), 2nd edn, 1986; cf. Bright, *Jeremiah*, CXXV-CXXXVIII. W.L. Holladay, 'The Recovery of Poetic Passages of Jeremiah', *JBL* 85, 1966, 401-35 analyzes prose bits of Jeremiah for traces of their original form. Problems of defining and analyzing biblical poetry are discussed in J.L. Kugel, *The Idea of Biblical Poetry: Parallelism and its*

History, Yale: Yale University Press, 1981. A brilliant discussion of the
history of the debate about the 'poetic' nature of the Bible is to be found in S.
Prickett, *Words and the Word: Language, poetics and biblical interpretation*,
Cambridge: Cambridge University Press, 1986.

The religious beliefs and practices attacked in 2-4 may represent the normal
syncretistic forms of Yahwism as practised in the pre-exilic temple cult of
Jerusalem and here denounced on behalf of a particular religious party. On
this, see:

> Barker, *The Older Testament, passim.*
> Garbini, *History & Ideology*, 52-65.
> Smith, *Palestinian Parties*, 11-42, 62-74.

On the vexed question of the traditional Jeremiah's relation to the so-called
deuteronomic reform of Josiah see Skinner, *Prophecy and Religion*, 89-107;
also Hyatt, 'Jeremiah and Deuteronomy', *JNES* 1, 1942, 156-73 (= Perdue &
Kovacs, 113-27). Very useful analyses of 14.1-15.4(9) appear in W.A.M.
Beuken & H.W.M. van Grol, 'Jeremiah 14,1-15,9: A Situation of Distress
and its Hermeneutics. Unity and Diversity of Form—Dramatic Development',
in Bogaert, 297-342; and M. Kessler, 'From Drought to Exile: A Morpho-
logical Study of Jer. 14.1-15.4', *Proceedings of the Society of Biblical
Literature*, 1972, 501-25.

The literature on the laments in the book of Jeremiah is vast and increasing
all the time; the commentaries should be consulted at the relevant sections
for discussion and bibliographies. The standard work is W. Baumgartner,
Die Klagegedichte des Jeremia (BZAW 32), Giessen: Alfred Töpelmann, 1917
(ET *Jeremiah's Poems of Lament*, Sheffield: Almond Press, 1988); cf.
Skinner, *Prophecy and Religion*, 201-30. Recent integrated readings of the
laments include A.R. Diamond, *The Confessions of Jeremiah in Context:
Scenes of Prophetic Drama* (JSOTS 45), 1987; and T. Polk, *The Prophetic
Persona: Jeremiah and the Language of the Self* (JSOTS 32), 1984; cf. M.S.
Moore, 'Jeremiah's Progressive Paradox', *Revue Biblique* 93, 1986, 386-414.
More comprehensive and technical treatments may be found in F.D.
Hubmann, *Untersuchungen zu den Konfessionen Jer. 11, 18-12, 6 und Jer.
15.10-21* (Forschung zur Bibel 30), Würzburg: Echter Verlag, 1978; and N.
Ittmann, *Die Konfessionen Jeremias: Ihre Bedeutung für die Verkündigung
des Propheten* (WMANT 54), Neukirchen-Vluyn: Neukirchener Verlag,
1981. For the laments as protests against suffering see H. Mottu, *Les
'Confessions' de Jérémie: Une protestation contre la souffrance* (Le monde de
la Bible), Genève: Labor et Fides, 1985; Mottu does not employ this insight
in the way I have in Chapter 5. The piety and spirituality of Jeremiah are
emphasized by S.H. Blank, *Jeremiah: Man and Prophet*, Cincinnati: Hebrew
Union College Press, 1961; and C. Conroy, 'Jeremiah and Sainthood',

Studia Missionalia 35, 1986, 1-40. H. Graf Reventlow, *Liturgie und prophetisches Ich bei Jeremia*, Gütersloh: Gütersloher Verlagshaus Gerd Mohn, 1963 treats the laments as utterances of Jeremiah the cult prophet in his role as representative of the people. Alternative voices and dissenting opinions from the majority viewpoint may be found in Carroll, *Chaos*, 107-30; *idem*, *Jeremiah*, 274-403; E. Gerstenberger, 'Jeremiah's Complaints: Observations on Jeremiah 15.10-21', *JBL* 82, 1963, 393-408; A.H.J. Gunneweg, 'Konfession oder Interpretation in Jeremiabuch', *Zeitschrift für Theologie und Kirche* 67, 1970, 395-416; J. Vermeylen, 'Essai de Redaktionsgeschichte des "Confessions de Jérémie"', in Bogaert, 239-70.

An early dating for 30-31 is maintained by N. Lohfink, 'Der junge Jeremia als Propagandist und Poet: Zum Grundstock von Jer. 30-31', in Bogaert, 351-68. On 31.31-34 see C. Levin, *Die Verheissung des neuen Bundes in ihrem theologie-geschichtlichen Zusammenhang ausgelegt* (FRLANT 137), 1985; cf. Bright, 'An Experiment in Hermeneutics: Jeremiah 31.31-34', *Interpretation* 20, 1966, 188-210.

For general treatments of the OAN genre see:

> D.L. Christensen, *Transformations of the War Oracle in OT Prophecy: Studies in the Oracles against the Nations* (Harvard Dissertations in Religion 3), Missoula: Scholars Press, 1975.

> R.E. Clements, *Prophecy and Tradition*, Oxford: Blackwell, 1975, 58-72.

> J.H. Hayes, 'The Usage of Oracles against Foreign Nations in Ancient Israel', *JBL* 87, 1968, 81-92.

On Jer. 46-51 in particular:

> H. Bardtke, 'Jeremia der Fremdvölkerprophet', *ZAW* 53, 1935, 209-39; *ZAW* 54, 1936, 240-62.

> Carroll, *Jeremiah*, 751-59 (general discussion), 759-856 (commentary).

On the OAN against Babylon (50-51):

> K.T. Aitken, 'The Oracles against Babylon in Jeremiah 50-51: Structures and Perspectives', *Tyndale Bulletin* 35, 1984, 25-63.

For a general treatment of Babylon see J. Oates, *Babylon* (Ancient Peoples and Places 94), London: Thames & Hudson, rev. edn, 1986, especially pp. 115-62 for the biblical period to the end of the great city of Babylon sometime in the second or third century CE.

6

THE
NARRATIVES

> The continuator of Jeremiah goes on heaping prophecy upon
> prophecy without any regard to dates, until at last, in chap. xxxviii
> (as if the intervening chapters had been a parenthesis), he takes up
> the thread dropped in chap. xxi.
>
> Baruch de Spinoza

SPINOZA'S OBSERVATION cannot be gainsaid. Apart from 37–44
(i.e. part IV) there is little concern with order, be it sequential or
chronological, in the editing of the book of Jeremiah. Often the
chronological confusion is caused by the editorial framework adding
a date by way of introducing a narrative which requires no dating to
be understood. More generally the lack of connectedness between
narratives (27–29 are exceptional in this respect) is caused by the
accumulation of disparate material between stories and by the
placement of pieces in relation to one another for reasons of shared
motifs or sentiments (e.g., the book of the restoration of the fortunes
in 30–31 would appear to follow on from the motif 'the good that I
will do to my people' in 29.32). The cycles of collected materials have
been analyzed in Chapter 5, and now it is the turn of the various
narratives and prose cycles to be treated. There is throughout the
book of Jeremiah a scattering of narratives which require to be
viewed together but which the editors have kept separate for reasons
beyond our knowledge. In treating them together here for convenience's
sake (like the laments scattered about 11–20) their separate placements
in the book must be kept in mind. The presence in Jeremiah of
overlapping but separate narratives (e.g. 7.1-7; 26.1-6) is also a
noteworthy feature of the book and cannot be ignored by reading
various texts in isolation from one another.

Narrated actions
Throughout Jeremiah there are a number of stories which represent

the speaker as acting in certain ways which constitute statements about certain events and situations. These actions, which have been categorized as 'symbolic' or 'magical' by various scholars, deserve to be treated together as an extensive source of special features in the book. They appear in every part of the book and often pose particularly difficult interpretative problems for the reader. Starting in 13.1-7, they are to be found in 16.1-4; 19.1-2, 10-11; 25.15-29; 27.1-7, 12; 28.10-11; 32.6-15; 35; 43.8-13; 51.59-64. We may also note the extended metaphors of 18.1-11 which share the common theme of pottery with 19.1-2, 10-11 and the visions (1.11-14; 24.1; 38.21-23), which also convey part of the book's teachings. With the exception of 32.6-15 every one of these actions purports the destruction of nation (Judean or foreign) or city (Jerusalem or Babylon); they thus reinforce the highly negative tenor of the book (the exception, 32.42-44, is a tacit acknowledgment of destruction which, however, refers to a later time). In 25.15-29; 43.8-13; 51.59-64 the destruction is posited of foreign nations, but only 51.59-64 (by implication of its *present* context following 50–51.58) allows for the corollary of Judah's deliverance. Two major problems make these narrated actions difficult to interpret: the nature of the actions and the narrative forms used in the book. Neither of these facets of the stories is as simple or as clear-cut as sometimes appears to be the case in the standard commentaries. Some of the stories are easier to understand than others (e.g. 32.6-15), but few of them are free of serious difficulties of interpretation. Thus they are very much part of the overall hermeneutical problems posed by the book of Jeremiah to the modern reader.

These strange actions in which the speakers behave in bizarre ways and attempt thereby to convey to an implied audience lessons amplifying their spoken words are a feature common to the books of Jeremiah and Ezekiel. Were these just actions symbolizing or accompanying words? Often the bizarreness of the action (cf. 25.15-17; 43.8-13; Ezek. 4.1-3, 4–8, 9-17; 5.1-8) or the length of its duration must have defeated any didactic purpose, especially as an audience for these events is presupposed only by the reader (19.1-2; 32.10-14 are exceptional in recognizing the need for witnesses). If these actions were performed in the presence of witnesses to whom explanations could be given, the text regularly fails to make that point, though it does include explanations of the significance of the actions (but to whom?). One way of explaining these actions is to place them against a background of ancient magical thinking and practice.

The ideological editors of the Hebrew Bible have tended to play down the legitimacy of magic in ancient Israel, so there is an equivalent tendency among modern interpreters to regard biblical activity as rational rather than magical or superstitious. This may be a grossly anachronistic reading of the Bible, especially of some of these narrated actions. The breaking of a ceramic flask outside the gates of Jerusalem and the utterance of a divine threat against that city (19.1-2, 10-11) have all the marks of an ancient execration ritual resonant with magical beliefs. Jeremiah's subsequent manhandling by the priestly authorities (20.1-2) hardly suggests a symbolic action with no force but is surely a recognition of the force of what had just been done, and of how the city's fate had been sealed by the action accompanied by the utterance of the divine name. A similar magical force would appear to lie behind the action in 51.59-64, where the spoken words are written down in a book which is then despatched to Babylon by an instructed delegate, where it is read out over the territory (or city?); after which the book has a stone bound to it and is cast into the depths of the river Euphrates. As the book sinks so will great Babylon sink, to rise no more! Dramatic, impressive, and profoundly magical (cf. the ritual of written curses washed into a cup of holy water and sanctuary dust, which constituted the ordeal test imposed by male jealousy on wives suspected of adultery in Num. 5.11-30).

Whether this world of magic is the necessary condition and background of all the narrated actions in the book of Jeremiah is debatable. Some of the actions may simply be symbolic; but it is very difficult to separate them from their setting in an ancient world where the magical and the superstitious are to be found everywhere. Most modern commentators on Jeremiah detect magical influences in 19.1-2, 10-11 and 51.59-64, though they tend towards a more rational explanation for the other actions. The lack of a comprehensive account of each action with its supporting warrants and reports of the reactions of witnesses (no exhaustive account of a narrated action is given in the text) makes it difficult for modern interpreters to be certain of what is going on in any one of the stories.

This point about the brevity and incompleteness of each account calls attention to the essential *narratedness* of what we possess in the text. Given the accounts as they appear in the written text, we face serious problems in trying to understand their nature. 32.6-15 is the least problematic of all the narrated actions, but it is exceptional in being relatively coherent and complete—though as is typical of the book of Jeremiah, it is expanded at great and irrelevant length in 32.16-41 until in vv. 42-44 its point is reiterated. 19.1-13 illustrates some of the difficulties both of the narratedness of the actions and the editing of the prose sections in the book of Jeremiah. The story of the action with the ceramic flask, involving the taking of leading citizens and priests beyond the gates of Jerusalem as witnesses to the smashing of the flask and the utterance of the divine words, has to be pieced together from a highly edited passage containing strands of a polemic against the cults of Jerusalem and the high places of Baal and the fire-cult of Topheth (cf. 7.31-34). There is *no* straightforward story of an action involving that purchased flask with its expedition out of the city. Any such story has been ruined by editorial insertions trying to link it with (deuteronomistic style) polemics against a number of disparate cults of an idolatrous nature. That is how the tradition has developed at this point; and we may speculate whether there was ever an initial stage of the tradition which consisted simply of an original narrated action. Such problems arise regularly with the text of Jeremiah and make the life of the modern exegete very difficult indeed! What can be said about this feature of Jeremiah is that it is very much a creation of the editors who put together and developed the text in such a way that what we now read represents a splicing together of a number of strands loosely presented as a unified narrative (cf. 26; 27; 29 for similar interweavings of various discrete and disparate strands).

When the reader asks the obvious question about these narrated actions—i.e. *'What is happening here?'*—it is not always easy to give a satisfactory reply. Consider the actions narrated in 13.1-7 and 25.15-17. 13.1-7 looks relatively simple: the speaker is commanded to go and buy (cf. 19.1) a linen girdle and to wear it without washing it; he then receives a second command to go to the Euphrates and there to bury the girdle among the rocks. Then after a long time he is commanded once again to return to Babylonia, to dig up the girdle, and to discover that it is ruined! Before asking the question *'what does that narrated action mean?'* (cf. vv. 8-11) the reader should note some serious problems of understanding raised by details in the story. These concern time, distances, and (the lack of) witnesses.

Examining such problems allows for an analysis of genre and interpretative modes required for reading such a story. The distance between Jerusalem and Babylon may be estimated at about four hundred miles across extremely rough terrain, and a journey there and back would encompass a few months at least. Two such trips separated by 'many days' would suggest a period of about a year for the action narrated in 13.1-7. Such distances and so much time (cf. Ezekiel's long stint of lying on one side in Ezek. 4) for an action make the question about witnesses all the more pertinent. The lack of witnesses to this rather extensive activity is notable (contrast 19.1; 32.10; 43.9). If there had been witnesses to it, what exactly would they have seen? A man walking about wearing an unwashed linen girdle for a period of time, then disappearing for months and returning without it for another period of time and then disappearing for months again until eventually he returned with a ruined girdle! Would they have noticed these things at all? So perhaps the absence of witnesses is a recognition of the kind of story this is. It is not the sort of action which can be witnessed and it is perhaps also not an act to be understood literally in the first place. A few brave scholars read the story literally, even though travel to Babylon was hazardous at the best of times; and some try to save the appearances by understanding the Hebrew word for the Euphrates (*perat*) as a reference to Parah, a town near Anathoth (cf. Josh. 18.23; Bright). The story could, of course, be simply a literary parable which only existed in speech or writing without ever having had any realistic activity behind it. It could have been a vision (cf. Rudolph, 93) of which this is the report, though no editorial indications are given to warrant this interpretation. The text simply reports the action as the speaker's response to divine commands, and thereby poses many problems of genre and analysis for the modern reader.

The meaning of the narrated action provided by the editors in vv. 8-11 is couched in deuteronomistic language, and relates the parable to the pride or idolatry of Judah and Jerusalem. It is not easy to see how this meaning can be derived from the details given in the narrative, but allowance should be made for significant gaps between story and meaning in the Bible (cf. the parables of Jesus and their interpretations in the Gospels). The *two* nations as the girdle worn by Yahweh makes an awkward metaphor (made awkward by the probable addition in v.11 of the phrase 'the whole house of Israel and'), but the explanation does connect up with the story to some extent. The ruining of the garment by the deliberate policy of the speaker and its burial in Babylonia are less easily explained in the terms suggested by vv. 9-10. Was Judah ruined by exile to Babylon, and, if so, what had idolatry to do with it? Did the Babylonians ruin Judah by invasion or by the importation of their culture to Judah? Just how precise is the match between vv. 8-11 and vv. 1-7? Here we have in a nutshell the interpretative problems involved in any reading of the text of Jeremiah. Every analysis and each answer offered by exegetes flounders owing to the lack of sufficient data in the text. To make coherent sense of the passage requires importing extraneous material into the text and imposing on it a genre which cannot be determined from the text itself. These two activities render all subsequent interpretations open to serious question and inevitably demonstrate the problematic nature of the narrated actions in the book of Jeremiah.

Equally difficult is the narrated action of 25.15-17 (27-29). Again the speaker is commanded to do things: to take from Yahweh's hand a cup of wine (symbolizing wrath) and to make all the nations drink it in order to become drunk. The speaker obeys the command and makes the nations drink the wine. But *what* can be meant by this action? The term 'hand of Yahweh' is not a literal one but a figure of speech; are then the other terms in v. 15 also figures of speech? *Gods do not hand goblets of wine down from the heavens to humans*, so we are bound to understand this fragment of narrative as a non-literal event. Is it then a parable, an allegory, a vision, a drama, a literary fable or what? No clues are provided by the text other than the stereotyped editorial framework rubric 'thus Yahweh, the god of Israel, said to me' (cf. 13.1; 16.1; 19.1). It is reported speech; but of what is it a report? Editorially the narrated action is supplemented by a long list of nations (vv. 19-26) and further elements of the action (vv. 27-28) with an explanation of why it is happening (v. 29). If vv. 19-26 are taken literally, the distances of 13.1-7 pale into a mere stroll; and we must envisage the speaker wandering from nation to nation with that mug of wine over many years! Clearly a literary or metaphorical understanding of the text is a requirement of modern exegesis. Part of the problem lies in the text as edited (i.e., action plus list) and its lack of clear and comprehensive details. Most of Jeremiah suffers from these problems, so every suggestion made by modern readers may be reasonable or intelligent but cannot command the assent of all readers. Confining oneself to the text cripples interpretation! Yet if sense is to be made of the story, some framework of reference must be supplied in which to read the text. Some exegetes have suggested reading many of these narrated actions as street theatre or dramatic actions (rather than as magical practices), and good sense can sometimes be produced by this approach. It does, however, assume an inordinate amount of background information which cannot be substantiated from any source.

This rather long consideration of only a few elements in only one strand of narrative in Jeremiah is intended to focus the reader's attention on the complexities involved in the reading of such texts. A book-length treatment would be justified on the 'symbolic' or 'magical' acts in Jeremiah and the background information necessary for understanding them. These kinds of story are not like the rationality of one of Plato's dialogues or the scepticism of Socrates in which each stage of the argument is carefully put forward and exhausted in discussion. The Bible is very unlike such rational discourses. It frequently uses metaphors and images, wordplays and oracles, and constantly so in Jeremiah; but few of these are ever expanded or explained in such rational terms that the modern reader can grasp them without ambiguity. It is simply not possible to free the biblical stories from such ambiguity, and nowhere is this more clearly the case than in the narrated actions of the book of Jeremiah.

7.1-15/26/36

Some of the editorial complexities in Jeremiah may be observed in the way in which various narratives are reused in the book or have links with other narratives. These are not stories placed side by side, yet they have clear connections with each other. The temple sermon in 7.1-7 reappears, under different circumstances, in 26.1-6 (v. 6 summarizes 7.8-15 in terms of 7.13-15), which develops the story along the lines of an imaginary tribunal. The highly structured account of Jeremiah before the people, princes, priests and prophets in 26.7-24 has clear echoes in 36 where the scroll of his words encounters many of these social strata. 36 in turn has parallels with

25.1-7 (especially 36.1-3) and with 2 Kings 22. It is not good exegesis to ignore all these interconnections, though space tends to curb comprehensive treatment of any of them.

The importance of the interconnectedness of these stories lies in the way it reveals the techniques of the creators of the book of Jeremiah. These are the ways in which they developed the material at their disposal or created new contexts for pieces of a storyline. The temple sermon of 7.1-15 is *not* the same as that given in 26 because there a socio-political setting is provided, and the social responses to the preaching are the dominant concern of the story. No reactions are provided to anything in the cycle of 7.1–8.3, whereas in parts III and IV Jeremiah is presented as being in dialogue with various strata of society. The editing of 26 places the sermon in the beginning of Jehoiakim's reign (26.1; perhaps influenced by 27.1; 28.1; 29.1?) and highlights this setting in vv. 20-23. But that king is entirely absent from the story! When we turn to 36, which is also set in king Jehoiakim's reign, we find that Jeremiah is absent throughout the three readings of the scroll of his words, but that on the third reading that king is very much present. Should then 26 and 36 be read in conjunction? They stand respectively at the beginning and ending of part III; is there then more to these stories than meets the eye at first reading? In 26 Jeremiah escapes with the help of Ahikam; in 36 he escapes (the same king's wrath) because he is in hiding. In 26 he has had his prophetic status affirmed by the princes and the people; in 36 Yahweh affirms the status of his words by ordering a rewritten scroll. In condemning Jeremiah and burning the scroll the king has condemned himself, his people and the city to destruction. 26.17-19 offers two paradigms of responding to the prophetic word and hints at how Jehoiakim responds to prophets (vv. 20-23); and in 36 Jehoiakim's reactions to Jeremiah's words (which he never hears in 26) confirm the analysis of 26.20-23. What in 26 may have represented a possibility of national turning back to Yahweh has become by 36 a definite refusal to turn. The fate of the nation was sealed by 36. Now we know the outcome of the conditional-absolute sermons of 7.1-15: the amendment of life possibility (7.5-7; 26.3-6) failed, so the word of absolute judgment must now be heard (cf. 37.1-2).

27-29

A special cycle of 'against the prophets' material appears in 27–29. This represents an independent cycle of narratives in the book: variations in the Hebrew spelling of proper names (e.g. Nebuchadnezzar for Nebuchadrezzar; *yirmᵉyâh* 'Jeremiah' for the normal *yirmᵉyāhû*; similar *-yâh* for *-yāhû* ending of Zedekiah), the naming of prophets other than Jeremiah and editorial dating which sets the stories in the same period are all features which set the cycle apart from other collections and blocks in the book. Each narrative, though built up out of edited units, includes attacks on prophets other than Jeremiah *the* prophet (MT). 27.2-3 provides a fragment of a narrated action, Jeremiah making yoke-bars, which is taken up in 28.10-11 but which allows for two versions of the action. Yoke-bars are made and worn by Jeremiah in 27.2, but in the Hebrew of 27.3 it is quite clear that he sends them to the kings of the neighbouring countries (this is corrected by RSV just as the EVV also correct 'Jehoiakim' in 27.1 to 'Zedekiah' to fit in with v. 12; cf. 28.1). Whether the wearing and making story is the original one or has developed from 28.10-11 is a moot point. The polemic against the prophets includes foreign prophets belonging to the neighbouring states (27.8-11), though the central concern of the cycle is the denigration of Judean prophets, whether in Jerusalem (27.14-22; 28) or Babylon (29.1, 9, 21-23, 31-32). In 27 and 28 that polemic is focused on a debate about the fate of the temple furnishings, an issue which has left its mark on a number of biblical stories (e.g. 2 Kgs 24.11-17; 25.13-17; Ezra 1.7; 2 Chron. 36.7, 10, 18; Dan. 1.2; 5.2-4; Isa. 52.11). In 28 and 29 the polemic focuses more on the question of a return of the exiles from Babylon (LXX 27 has the same theme).

The polemic between Jeremiah and the prophets in 27–29 is very different from the attack on and dismissal of prophets in 23.9-40, though the two sets of texts should be considered together as they share the same obsession with denunciation of the prophets. Where the difference between the two lies is in the denunciation of *all* the prophets in 23 whereas 27–29, in the second edition, denounce all the prophets *except Jeremiah the prophet* (in LXX he is not a prophet). Also 27–29 use narratives where 23 uses a collection of poetic and prose pieces. The quarrel between Jeremiah and Hananiah is unusual in this book and is strange in the light of the blanket condemnation of prophets given in 27 against those who maintain what Hananiah asserts in 28.2-4! Encounters between prophets seldom occur in the Bible at the level of two individuals in conflict (only here and 1 Kgs 13; 22), but where they do they are very complex narratives. 28 may look simple, but it is far from easy to discern what is going on in the chapter. Although many commentators read the story as the account of an historical encounter between two names prophets, it is better read as an ideological narrative in which the truth of Jeremiah's position is predetermined by editorial control. That control can be seen in the exchange between the two prophets in vv. 2-4, 5-9, where a distinction is made between prophets who declare war against great kingdoms and those who prophesy peace (*šālôm*). Such a differentiation is intended to mark off Jeremiah from Hananiah, yet on reflection is it not the case that Hananiah also has spoken war against the great kingdom of Babylon? Is he not therefore in the godly company of the prophets who preceded him and Jeremiah? Of course he is! But what makes him exceptional here and puts him in the wrong is the fact that his story is told in the context of a pro-Babylonian cycle of material. He therefore must not speak against the great empire (servant of Yahweh according to 27.5-7!) as if he were a genuine prophet rooted in the tradition of war prophets! That ideological determination of story by context destroys Hananiah, and at the end of 28 he is dead (contrast 26.24 where at the end of 26 Jeremiah is *not* dead, and compare 29.32 where Shemaiah and his family face death at the end of that story).

The pro-Babylonian politics of the cycle continue in 29 where the deported people are encouraged by a letter from Jeremiah to settle down in Babylonia and there create for themselves a normal life (vv. 4-7). The permanence of this life in Babylon is shown by their building houses, planting gardens and settling down into married life: all long-term enterprises bespeaking the permanent settlement of Judeans in Babylon. Prayers are even to be made for the wellbeing (*šālôm*) of Babylon (v. 7) for the obvious reason that the welfare of the Babylonian city will determine the wellbeing of the Judeans. Such a letter reflects the permanence of life in Babylon and speaks against those prophets, whether in Judah or Babylon, who were agitating for a return of the exiles to Jerusalem. 29 is another good example of the complexities of editing in the production of Jeremiah: it is a chapter full of disparate pieces which are only unified by the motif 'against the prophets'. The letter of vv. 4-7 must be regarded as ending there because the rest of the chapter is a series of disjunctive responses to various activities rather than a continuation of the letter (cf. vv. 24-28 which seem to cite the letter of vv. 4-7 and therefore cannot be part of that letter!). The polemic against the prophets in vv. 8-9 is disrupted by a piece in vv. 10-14 about the return from Babylon (an addition reflecting 25.11, 14; 27.7?) and is then continued in v. 15 only to be disrupted by vv. 16-19 before being completed by vv. 20-23 (in a manner of speaking). This haphazard way of editing the chapter may reflect important concerns of the editors of the section, but it does not contribute to clarity of understanding on the reader's part. Once again the nature of the editing must determine the way we read the material rather than what sense may be derived from its constituent pieces. The overriding concern of the editors in 27-29 is to denounce the prophets other than Jeremiah, and everything else is secondary to that motive.

34/35

These two chapters are set in the reigns of different kings (chronologically reversed!) but they have certain links between each other. 34.8-22 is about a covenant made between Zedekiah and the people in Jerusalem, and 35 is about a group of people living in Jerusalem who have been faithful to their ancestor's command. The connection between the two stories, apart from their being together in part III, is the way they reflect on the nature of commitment and fidelity to commands. In 34 the covenant which freed the slaves is renegued by king and slave-owners, and this reneguing is symbolic of the nation's rejection of the covenant made when the fathers came out of Egypt (vv. 12-14) as well as being a rejection of a sacred covenant made in the temple (vv. 15-16). 35 is set in the temple and is another narrated action in which Jeremiah attempts to corrupt the Rechabites by making them drink wine when they are known to be a community which rejects viticulture and other settled agricultural activities. Their loyalty to the ancient command not to drink wine nor to settle in houses is a contrasting symbol of the nation's failure to be loyal to the divine command. Set together like this the stories are inevitably read as a study in contrasting attitudes to the past and to clan loyalty as well as a further set of explanations for the destruction of Jerusalem.

21.1-10/34.1-7/37/38

These sections may be read together because they are linked by a
number of similar motifs, and especially in relation to the motif
'Jeremiah and Zedekiah'. The stories in 34, 37, 38 are interviews
between the prophet and the king; but 21.1-10 should be considered
here because it shares the motif of the delegation sent by Zedekiah to
Jeremiah with 37. 37 and 38 are variations of the same story. Taken
together, all four pieces provide an interesting set of variations on the
theme of Jeremiah and Zedekiah. Repetition and variety characterize
the telling of these stories, and each one has differences which
contribute to a variegated pattern of representation of the dealings
between king and prophet. The tenor of defeat by the Babylonians is
common to all versions of the storytelling, though 38.17 moots the
possibility of escape for king and city. 34.4-5 introduces a strange
note into what is otherwise a collection of notices of doom in that it
speaks of a peaceful (*šālôm*) death followed by the usual pomp of
state obsequies. This is similar to 2 Kgs 22.20 but runs counter to the
information provided about the fate of Zedekiah in 39.5-7; 52.9-11.
The delegation motif in 37.3-10 is quite unlike its version in 21.1-10
where it is developed into a structured gradation of survival
possibilities. That possibility of survival is also part of the background
to the interview motif in 38 where it accounts for Jeremiah's
imprisonment in a cistern (vv. 1-7). In 37 he is imprisoned as a result
of being caught leaving the city during a lull in the siege (vv. 11-15).

Although the themes of delegation or interview run through these
stories there is no consistent line taken which would provide a
coherent and consistent account of Jeremiah and Zedekiah. The
hostility of the deuteronomists to Zedekiah (e.g. 39.5-7; 52.1-3) is,
however, hardly characteristic of the stories in 34, 37, 38 (21.7
probably reflects deuteronomistic hostility also). In the interviews
Jeremiah and Zedekiah behave in a reasonably friendly way towards
each other, but this may reflect the storytelling more than anything
else. However, all the stories should be read as an exercise in
observing how variety and detail are incorporated into a pattern of
stories built around the simple theme of 'Jeremiah and Zedekiah'.
There are no encounters between Jeremiah and other kings (in spite
of the listing of kings in 1.2-3), and the hostility displayed by the
cycle in 21.11-23.6 (in its highly edited form) is remarkably absent
from the portrayal of Jeremiah in conversations with Zedekiah.

From the viewpoint of part IV Zedekiah is the only king with whom Jeremiah had any personal contact. Whether that feature warrants the inference that Jeremiah was not active in the time of Jehoiakim, except in the editorial framework, is a much disputed point.

38/39/40.1-6
38 has links with 39 in that the figure of the Ethiopian official introduced as the rescuer of Jeremiah from the cistern in 38.7-13 reappears in 39.15-18 in terms which have links with 21.9 and 45.5. 37.21; 38.13, 28 tie in with 39.15 and illustrate how 37–39 are really of a piece under the general rubric 'the fall of Jerusalem', though the linkages with other sections of Jeremiah can be made in a variety of ways. Little is said in the Hebrew Bible about the details of the Babylonian destruction of Jerusalem, and what is given tends to be a variation on the deuteronomistic accounts in 2 Kgs 24–25. 39.1-10 (cf. 52.3b-11) provides a textually confused account (much of it is not in the LXX) of the last moments of the city and the fate of Zedekiah and the people. In 39.11-14 and 40.1-6 two different stories are given about the fate of Jeremiah. 37-38 have explained how Jeremiah survived through the days of famine caused by the siege (37.21); now there are two accounts of how he escaped from the doomed city and lived to see another day. In one story Nebuchadrezzar, the Babylonian emperor, makes it his personal business to have Jeremiah well looked after. The other story has him being taken to Babylon in chains and being released in mid-journey by Nabuzaradan, captain of the guard (or butchers), and sent back to his homeland. The net result of these two stories is that Jeremiah survives the fall of Jerusalem and settles down in the Judean territory to live in the community run by the pro-Babylonian Gedaliah (son of the man who had rescued him from the mob in 26.24?).

40.7–41.18
Taken together the pieces here constitute the story of Gedaliah's community in the aftermath of the fall of Jerusalem. It is a strange section in the book of Jeremiah because *Jeremiah himself is entirely absent from the story*! The parallel account in 2 Kgs 25.22-26, a much briefer account of the collapse of Gedaliah's community, also lacks Jeremiah, but then the deuteronomistic history knows absolutely nothing of Jeremiah (or of any of the prophets except for the Isaiah of

2 Kgs 18-20 = Isa. 36-39). 40.7-41.18 looks like an expanded version of the details in 2 Kings 25, with additional material in 42-43.7 incorporating Jeremiah into the story. The absence of Jeremiah is only remarkable in the context of the book of Jeremiah and in the light of 42. However the matter is to be accounted for, the story of Gedaliah's brief organization of life in Palestine after the collapse of Jerusalem is told in terms of a community which knew not Jeremiah. Whether its disintegration because of that lack is a subtle point being made by the editors is a moot question, though such a view sounds too clever in the light of 42, where Jeremiah suddenly reappears. That absence of Jeremiah in 40.7-41.18 must be added to the complications of explaining how the book of Jeremiah was produced. The tale unfolded in this story is a sad one of social and political pressures causing the disruption of the nascent community and leading to the assassination of Gedaliah by forces resentful of his collaboration with the Babylonian authorities. As the story is told in 41 it is not easy to grasp how Ishmael and ten men were able to kill so many people, defeat the Babylonian garrison at Mizpah (41.3), and take captive the rest of the people. Whether there is anything historical at all about the story cannot be determined at this distance from the period, though certain general features in the account may be an accurate reflection of life in the Babylonian and Persian periods.

42-44

Jeremiah reappears in 42 as the prophet to whom the people turn in a time of grave crisis (but why not in 41?). After the death of Gedaliah Johanan assumed leadership of the community and in 40.7-43.7 he appears to be the effective leader much more than Gedaliah had been in his brief period of control. The Jeremiah of 42 is a man to whom the community resort for prayer and supplication, rather than as a prophet known for his proclamations of the divine word. He is not here the one to whom the divine word comes but one who must *wait* for that word (42.7; cf. 28.12); i.e., he is not a preacher so much as an expert in prayer (contrast 7.16; 11.14; 14.11). In a lengthy, deuter-onomistically influenced sermon he warns against going to Egypt and promises divine protection for the community if they stay in the land of Judah (42.9-12; v. 11 shares elements with 1.8, 19; 15.21a). This possibility of divine mercy in the homeland is in striking contrast to the anti-Judean propaganda of 24.8-10; 29.16-19 and hints at an alternative view of the homeland in the tradition. It is not developed because inveterate hatred of the Jews in Egypt and indeed of all things Egyptian takes over and dominates 42.13-22; 44. Jeremiah's counsel is rejected by a community (rightly) fearful of Babylonian retaliation for the slaughter of Babylonian soldiers (41.3). Baruch is blamed for this counsel (43.3)! Throughout 37–42 there is not a hint of Baruch's presence, let alone of his role as Jeremiah's counsellor; so perhaps here we have the beginnings of Baruch's rise to power in the story of Jeremiah (cf. 45; see Chapter 7 below). In 43.8-13 a narrated action conveys the message of Yahweh's hostility against Egypt. The lengthy 44 is made up of numerous (deuteronomistic) pieces of a prolix nature denigrating *all the Jewish communities throughout Egypt* (44.1): thus it cannot be read as a continuation of 43, where only one community retreats to Egypt. Such hostility against the Jews of Egypt bespeaks an ideological conflict between various Jewish communities, perhaps of the second temple period (Persian, Greek?), and reflecting profound tensions in the relation of Palestinian, Babylonian, and Egyptian Jews (see Chapter 8 below).

45

This brief fragment following 44 is not really a narrative but a lengthy editorial framework introduction setting it in 605 and therefore relating it to 36, an oracle addressed to Baruch(!) referring to a statement of his, and an oracle of response to him. In its five verses it raises more questions and interpretative problems than do most five-verse sections of the book. What looks like a brief lament in v. 3, quite different from anything in the laments in 11–20, with its directed response makes an interesting contrast with the complete lack of such edited connectedness (i.e., the speaker of the lament is identified, and complaint is directly responded to) in the poems of 11–20. Whatever may lie behind this brief chapter it is an interesting example of how at one or two points in the tradition the figure of Baruch is briefly glimpsed. Although not in chronological order, the placement of the piece after 44 may be a deliberate attempt to balance the awful finality of the annihilation of the Jews of Egypt. Baruch, now in Egypt, is to be a survivor in the coming disaster which will befall 'all flesh' (45.5). Like Jeremiah and Ebed-melech,

Baruch symbolizes survival in the future. Beyond that slight contrast with the slaughter implicit in 44 and characteristic of the closing decades of Judean national existence (45.1 is now dated to 605 by the editors), little can be said about 45 (see Chapter 9 below). With 45 part IV ends on a strange note uncharacteristic of a part of the book devoted entirely to the period of Jerusalem's fall and its aftermath; but by now the reader should not be surprised by anything encountered in the reading of the book of Jeremiah!

Further Reading

The citation from Spinoza's *Tractatus Theologico-Politicus* (1670) is taken from the translation by R.H.M. Elwes in *The Chief Works of Benedict de Spinoza* I, New York: Dover Publications, 1951, 148.

On the symbolic actions of the prophets see G. Fohrer, *Die symbolischen Handlungen der Propheten*, Zürich: Zwingli-Verlag, 1953, 2nd edn, 1968; J. Lindblom, *Prophecy in Ancient Israel*, Oxford: Blackwell, 1962, 137-48, 165-73; also S. Amsler, *Les actes des prophètes* (Essais bibliques 9), Genève: Labor et Fides, 1985; T.W. Overholt, 'Seeing is Believing: The Social Setting of Prophetic Acts of Power', *JSOT* 23, 1982, 3-31. On the street theatre approach to these acts see B. Lang, 'Street Theater, Raising the Dead, and the Zoroastrian Connection in Ezekiel's Prophecy', in J. Lust (ed.), *Ezekiel and his Book: Textual and Literary Criticism and their Interrelation* (BETL 74), Leuven: Leuven University Press, 1986, 297-307; *idem, Monotheism and the Prophetic Minority: An Essay in Biblical History and Sociology*, Sheffield: Almond Press, 1983, 83-91; cf. Carroll, *Chaos*, 130-35 on the prophet as actor.

On the individual narrated actions consult the commentaries at the relevant places.

On 13.1-11 see C.H. Southwood, 'The Spoiling of Jeremiah's Girdle (Jer. XIII 1-11)', *VT* 29, 1979, 231-37; on the possible background to 25.15-17 see W. McKane, 'Poison, Trial by Ordeal and the Cup of Wrath', *VT* 30, 1980, 474-92.

On parts III and IV see M. Kessler, 'Jeremiah 26–45 Reconsidered', *JNES* 25, 1968, 81-88.

For elements in 27–29 consult the commentaries and also P.R. Ackroyd, 'The Temple Vessels: A Continuity Theme', in *Studies in the Religious Tradition of the Old Testament* London: SCM Press, 1987, 46-60 (=*SVT* 23, 1972, 166-81); D. Lys, 'Jérémie 28 et le problème du faux prophète ou la circulation du sens dans le diagnostic prophétique', *Revue d'histoire et de philosophie religieuses* 59, 1979, 453-82.

On 37-44 see Ackroyd, 'Historians and Prophets', in *Studies*, 142-51 (=*Svensk Exegetisk Årsbok* 33, 1968, 18-54); on 45 see M.A. Taylor, 'Jeremiah 45: The Problem of Placement', *JSOT* 37, 1987, 79-98.

7

THE FIGURE
OF JEREMIAH

Jeremiah was truly the genius of torment and discord, the
Euripides, the Pascal or the Dostoyevsky of the Old Testament.

Jean Steinmann

RUNNING THROUGH THE BOOK of Jeremiah, especially in parts III
and IV and the prose elements of part I, are glimpses of the
figure of Jeremiah. To some extent this figure may be said to hold
together the disparate material constituting the book, though 40.7–
41.18 and 52, where Jeremiah is entirely absent, are clearly
exceptions to this claim. The 'I' and 'me' of various prose pieces are
assumed by most exegetes to represent Jeremiah as speaker, and the
editorial framework frequently attributes prose actions and statements
to him. Reading the book at face value and following the dictates of
traditional and conventional readings of the text, the bulk of modern
scholars have understood Jeremiah to be the book of the life and
times of Jeremiah the prophet, with direct access to his words, deeds,
innermost thoughts and reflections. Such an approach presupposes
so much historical information to which nobody has access and a
one-to-one correspondence between text and social reality that it is
an extremely problematical reading of the book. The precise relation
between the character constructed by the writers of the tradition and a
hypothesized 'historical' Jeremiah behind the book is a very difficult
question to answer, though not acknowledging its existence in the
first place does not make it any the less real a problem for
interpreting the book. For the purpose of this chapter the character
of Jeremiah presented in the book will be treated as the creative
fiction of the editors and writers who produced it and the relation
between the 'historical' Jeremiah and the 'fictional' Jeremiah will be
left to the speculative sophistications of the reader.

The biographical reading of Jeremiah may be found in most books
on Jeremiah and is well championed by so many scholars (e.g. Bright,

Berridge, Holladay, Thompson etc.) that it hardly needs repeating
here. It consists of simply reading the book of Jeremiah as a literal
account of the life and times of Jeremiah the prophet and reconstructing
suitable social settings for his work in order to produce a biographical
interpretation of the work. Traditionally this has entailed placing
Jeremiah's birth in the 650/640 BCE period and his call to be a
prophet in the thirteenth year of Josiah (i.e. 627/6) following the
conjunction of 1.2 and 1.5. The reference to 'youth' in 1.6-7 is taken
literally rather than as a metaphor or conventional reference to
inexperience or deference (cf. 1 Kgs 3.7). More recently there has
been a tendency to question the dating of Jeremiah's call to the year
627/6 because little that is regarded as belonging to the authentic
words of Jeremiah can be assigned to the time of Josiah. Some
exegetes would understand the date in 1.2 to be that of Jeremiah's
birth (e.g. Holladay, 14–17) and would adjust the period of his
ministry accordingly, though Holladay would still make him a
youthful prophet and assign some of his work to the time of Josiah.
These are minor adjustments in ways of reading the text literally
while persisting with a biographical interpretation of Jeremiah. They
make no allowance for the highly edited nature of ch. 1 nor for the
use of metaphor and convention in 1.4–10, and are therefore open to
serious questioning about their adequacy as readings of complex
texts.

A more serious approach to ch. 1 and a more satisfactory reading
of it appear in McKane's commentary (pp. 1-25). He takes full
cognizance of the untidiness of the text and the shaping influences of
the editors in its construction, so that the biographical reading of it
disappears. Positing an exilic or post-exilic dating for the chapter is
also more sensible given McKane's reading of it. For my part I would
have to say that the following representations of Jeremiah are the
main elements in the book. Taken together, they appear to contribute
to a biographical account of the speaker behind the tradition. But
this is so unusual in the books collected together in the 'latter
prophets' (i.e. Isaiah to Malachi), where the figure of the speaker is
almost invariably absent (a few chapters in Isaiah, the representation
of the 'son of man' character in Ezekiel, Hos. 1; 3; Amos 7.10-15 may
be exceptions or may be patient of different explanations), that it
would be wise to resist the temptation to rush into reading the book
of Jeremiah as if it were an early version of autobiographical sketches

from ancient Judah! Although the majority of scholars continue to read Jeremiah as a biographical or autobiographical set of documents, and this 'compact majority' must be recognized for whatever value may be attached to such statistical reports, we cannot prejudge the issue as if there were no alternative or more feasible accounts of how the book was put together. Such accounts undergird the logic of the claim that perhaps *the figure of Jeremiah is more the creation of the tradition than the creator of it.*

1. Jeremiah the prophet

The phrase 'Jeremiah *the prophet*' has already been noted as a feature of part IV and as very much part of the development of the second edition now represented by the MT. It may have been in the period between the production of the two editions, perhaps in quite different locations, that the view of Jeremiah as a prophet became a dominant motif of the tradition. The roots of that motif are present in one set of narratives common to both editions, but what this represents cannot be stated with any certitude. A number of other elements in the book may serve as ramifications of that motif (e.g. the narrated actions discussed in Chapter 6), though the literary and interpretative problems associated with them make the reinforcement of Jeremiah's prophetic status a good deal less persuasive than some scholars seem to think the case to be. The point being made here is important: where there are interpretative difficulties in handling textual pieces and where no one interpretation is unproblematical, it is not possible to assume these pieces into a straightforward, simple account of the meaning of the book. Economy of explanation is a good principle but it cannot be used to conceal textual ambiguities and other difficulties. The many passages of narrated actions in Jeremiah are a good example of this important point and, although they are often read as simple presentations of the prophetic status of Jeremiah, must be treated with the caution appropriate to reading complex texts. It may well be the case that such narrated actions indicate the development of the 'Jeremiah-as-a-prophet' stage of the tradition's growth, a stage similar in many ways to the stories about prophets incorporated into Samuel-Kings and Chronicles. But such stages are features of the editing of the book and do not necessarily throw any light on the substantive contents of the text.

The introductory colophon prefaces the book with the phrase 'the words of Jeremiah. . . ' (cf. Amos 1.1; Eccl. 1.1) which is then expanded by the secondary v. 2 linking his words with 'the word of Yahweh'; this in turn makes connections with 1.4, 7, 8, 11, 13; 2.1, 2, 3, 4 which all relate to the divine word being received by Jeremiah (named in 1.1, 11). Undoubtedly the editors of the book present Jeremiah as one who receives the divine words: this is done by means of the prologues (2.1-4 as much as ch. 1) which condition the reading (and hearing) of the book as the work of a prophetic speaker. This prophetic status is explicitly acknowledged in 1.5 with the phrase 'a prophet to the nations'. Absolutely nothing in 1 or 2.1-4 indicates a date for the creation of these pieces, so arguments for the dating of Jeremiah's activity *as a prophet* are inevitably extra-textual. Whether 1 should be viewed as exilic or post-exilic in construction (cf. McKane, *Jeremiah*, 25) is a very difficult matter to determine, but in view of 1.3 which presupposes the fall of Jerusalem, and 1.5 which appears to assume 25.15-38 and the OAN (46–51), some of which presuppose the fall of Babylon, a post-exilic date for the chapter seems the more likely possibility. But there are no knockdown arguments in the matter of dating individual chapters, so scholars must work with certain assumptions based on the tenor of the book or certain sections of it.

Here a book-length argument would be required to tease out all the implications of how *different readings* of the text produce very different understandings of Jeremiah's status as a prophet. Working from the more conventional and traditional readings of the book as the work of a prophet makes many of the stories very difficult to understand: e.g. Jeremiah is acknowledged as one who speaks the word of Yahweh to the *princes* and *all* the people (26.16) and *commands elders* of the people and senior *priests* (19.1) to accompany him on some of his missions. If these stories genuinely reflect his status as a prophet of Yahweh in Jerusalem society before the destruction of the city by the Babylonians, how can the book also argue that people, princes and priests rejected his preaching and thus brought the catastrophe on themselves? Surely confusion and contradiction are entailed here! If, on the other hand, a different approach to the text is taken and it is argued that the concern of the writers is to do two contradictory things, namely justify Jeremiah as a true prophet and *at the same time* condemn the people and the leaders for rejecting his prophetic status (cf. 36), then a very different kind of explanation becomes available for the text. Public support of Jeremiah the prophet and public rejection of him can only be sustained at a theoretical or *textual* level. That is, only in texts and stories can these incompatibilities be justified *and not in real life*. The writers must *do* two things: they must establish the status of Jeremiah as a true prophet, recognized by the people as such because without public recognition he cannot have been a true prophet, yet they must also account for the historical reality of the fall of Jerusalem in 587. Now if the people did accept Jeremiah as a genuine prophet they would have believed him and, according to the book's claims and values, the destruction of Jerusalem would have been averted. This did not happen, so it must have been the case that the people rejected the preaching of Jeremiah (cf. 2 Chron. 36.12). Hence the stories in the book which alternate between presenting Jeremiah as one who commands a following in the community which recognizes the truth of what he says, and the representation of the popular rejection of his preaching (contrast 26.16 with 36.31). The heart of the problem lies in the editorial values embodied in the book.

Something of the complexity of the arguments involved in arguing about the strand of the text which presents Jeremiah as a prophet should now be apparent to the reader. Only the limitations of space here prevent the full complexities of the matter from being investigated. When it is remembered that there is a significant difference between the distribution throughout the text of the epithet 'Jeremiah *the prophet*' in the first and second editions of the book, then the argument that Jeremiah *qua* prophet is part of the interpretative categories used by the producers of the text (rather than a reflection of the 'historical' Jeremiah) is strengthened. Perhaps now we can see that some of the stories have been constructed to support the beliefs of a later period about Jeremiah and that in the second edition the tradition has been enhanced to bear testimony to Jeremiah's status *as a prophet*.

Some traces of this development may be detected in the use of the technical phrase 'says Yahweh' (*nᵉ'um yhwh*) which is scattered throughout the book and used more frequently in the second edition. Both editions carry the phrase a great number of times, and often its use is quite redundant. Where the phrase is additional to the MT it is arguable that the second edition simply developed (or alternatively, belonged to circles where such a reading—or liturgical use?—was more common) what was already inherent in the tradition, namely the propensity to understand much of the tradition as oracular. The phrase is a technical reference to the oracular nature of an utterance and is used throughout the Hebrew Bible to indicate that a piece of text is believed to be a divine statement mediated via a legitimate channel of revelation. At times in Jeremiah it is used to punctuate statements introduced by the other technical phrase 'thus says Yahweh', and in such contexts appears surplus to requirements (e.g. 18.5; 30.17). Perhaps this punctuating use of it points to ligurgical or editorial developments of the text, as well as indicating the growth of the tradition in terms of the divinely spoken word category.

It cannot be denied that very many of the poems in the book are introduced by the stereotyped phrases indicative of oracular speech (e.g. 6.9, 16, 22; 9.7, 17, 20; 10.18; 13.15; 18.13), though in many cases the introductory formula could be removed without affecting the poem at all. This may or may not signal an editing of the poems within the framework of a general ideology of the tradition as the mediation of the divine word. That word may be communicated anonymously as easily as by named people. Whether then the attribution of the poems to Jeremiah by means of the editorial framework is a further stage in the development of the book or lay at the roots of the creation of the tradition must be a question to ponder rather than to answer. The argument here is tending in the direction of the claim that the oracular nature of much in the book is secondary in the sense of belonging to the stages of its editorial construction, and the extent to which the oracular may be traced back to before such edited levels is now impossible to determine. It need not be denied that some of the poems had their origins in oracular proclamations about invasion and destruction, but it would not follow that the editorial attribution (in the most general sense) of these utterances to Jeremiah necessarily reflects historically reliable information. Rather, the oracular nature of some of the poems and also of various edited levels of the text combined with the introduction of narratives featuring Jeremiah as an actor performing in many different ways served to accelerate the development of the 'fictional' prophet Jeremiah. We cannot step outside the pages of the text into history and assume that what may be true in the text is therefore also necessarily the case outside the text. *There is no 'outside the text'*! That is what the literariness of the Bible means; and all discussion in this book of the prophet Jeremiah is concerned with the literary Jeremiah, not with a hypothesized historical character. The fact that so many traditionalist scholars would dissent from this analysis may be noted and recorded as readings of the text on the assumption that it mirrors, in well- or ill-defined ways, social and historical reality. This sharp division of opinion about the nature of the biblical text is part of a much larger argument which cannot be pursued here, but its contours certainly help to define the way the text is read. In the presentation of the figure of Jeremiah in the book of Jeremiah, irrespective of what the historical and social connections may have been, the role of prophet is the most dominant one. That much may be freely granted. Little else in the arguments is as assured!

2. Jeremiah the priest

1.1 with its statement 'the words of Jeremiah the son of Hilkiah, of the priests who (was/were) in Anathoth in the land of Benjamin' is rather ambiguous. Whatever the original form of the title (e.g. simply 'the words of Jeremiah son of Hilkiah' or even 'the words of Jeremiah': cf. Amos 1.1) and its subsequent development, the present title allows one to deduce that Jeremiah was among the priests in Anathoth *or* that Hilkiah was one of the priests there and therefore nothing is said about Jeremiah's own priesthood (assuming that all sons of priests were not priests automatically?). The Targum reads 'the words of the prophecy of Jeremiah the son of Hilqiah, one of the leaders of the course of the priests, of the temple officers who were in Jerusalem: the man who received his inheritance in Anathoth in the land of the tribe of Benjamin'. (The paraphrastic and ideological nature of the Aramaic translation-interpretation should be obvious from this citation.) The Targum to Lam. 1.1 refers to Jeremiah as 'the great priest', thus drawing from the text and tradition one obvious inference. Was Jeremiah then a priest as well as a prophet? Here the evidence from the book of Jeremiah is much more inferential than that for the presentation of him as a prophet. In the Hebrew Bible the two roles can be interchangeable (especially in the case of Samuel and in the book of Chronicles), so the question is well worth raising about Jeremiah.

A number of the prose narratives represent Jeremiah as working in or from the temple; and this location of him there may imply for him a role as a cult prophet or even as a priest. He is certainly represented as making pronouncements about such priestly concerns as sacrifice (e.g. 6.20; 7.17-19, 21-24, 31-33; 11.15) and altars (17.1-2), though many scholars have read these references as being deuteronomistic constructs. The temple sermon of 7.1-15 (cf. 26) is preached in the gate (courtyard, 26.2) of the temple, though later in 36.5 he is debarred from the temple (a disgraced priest? the text offers no clues for this disbarment). In 35.2 he is commanded to *bring* the Rechabites to the temple where, in what may have been the chambers of a prophetic guild (35.4), he performs for them his action with cups of wine. The plain meaning of 29.26-27 is that Jeremiah is a prophet (or a madman playing the prophet!) in the temple (as in 28.5). We do not know whether prophets who were not members of guilds of cult prophets had access to the temple, though it should be recognized that it is the editors who repeatedly place Jeremiah in the temple where it would be natural *for them* to find him (cf. 2 Kgs 23.2 with 2 Chron. 34.30; see the role of Jehaziel in 2 Chron. 20.13-17). In 24.1 the speaker has a vision of baskets of figs set down *before the temple*, but little may follow from this temple reference. The complicated narrative-sermon of 19.1-15 has Jeremiah (named in v. 14) go out to one of the city gates; when he returns in v. 14 he stands in the temple courtyard, which rather suggests (if anything may be suggested by so complex a text as 19!) that he had gone out from the temple *in the first place*! In 18.1-2 Jeremiah is commanded to *go down* to the potter's house and in 22.1 to *go down* to the royal palace; now from 26.10; 36.11 we know that the relation of palace to temple was one of upper and lower levels, so that one went *up* to the temple and *down* to everywhere else. Thus the movements of Jeremiah in these stories are *from the temple* to places outside the temple precincts. Always he seems to be located in the temple or intimately connected with it, so we may conclude that from the editors' viewpoint he is a temple figure and therefore conceivably a priest, certainly a cult prophet. This then is the logic of his belonging to the priests in Anathoth.

There is in the book of Jeremiah sufficient allusion to the temple location of Jeremiah's activities to warrant the view that the editors regarded him as a figure connected with the cult. Whether as priest and/or cult prophet is more difficult to say. Again it must be emphasized that this temple role for the figure of Jeremiah in the book is a statement about the character depicted in the book and not firm information about a supposedly 'historical' Jeremiah. The priestly status of Jeremiah is a minor and somewhat inferential feature of the book depending to some extent on 1.1. It is nothing like the dominance of priestly elements and values in the book of Ezekiel. Yet it has a certain logic to it because the prophet Jeremiah must have exercized his ministry *somewhere* and gained his living (32.9 depicts him as a man of money, and buying things seems to be characteristic of him; e.g. 13.1; 19.1; 32.7) by some means. Where and how the book does not tell us: note the complete absence of location or setting for 1.4-10! The temple and its official ministries (priest, prophet, administrator etc) would therefore provide the most obvious context of his work (the domination of royal theology which permeates the book of Isaiah is so absent from Jeremiah that the prophet cannot be envisaged as a court official). He is certainly depicted as a priest in the extra-biblical literature, where he offers sacrifice in the temple over a period of time including the day of Atonement (e.g. Paraleipomena of Jeremiah; this book calls him 'Jeremiah the priest'). The beginnings of his role as priest may be detected in 1.1 and in the various stories where the editors have located him in the temple.

3. Jeremiah the actor

The narratives depicting the magical, symbolic and didactic activities of Jeremiah have been discussed in Chapter 6, though there the focus was on the interpretative problems of determining genre and meaning. Assuming for the sake of argument that actions, of whatever kind, are implied by such passages as 13.1-7; 19.1-2, 10-11; 25.15-17; 27.1-7, 12; 28.10-11; 32.6-15; 35; 43.8-13; 51.59-64, we may regard the figure of Jeremiah depicted throughout the book as a performer among the people. Whether these performances are to be understood as a primitive form of Hebrew (street) theatre or as acting in a more general sense must be left open because we have no evidence to warrant firm conclusions.

Bernhard Lang, speaking of Ezekiel, makes far too strong a claim when he asserts:

> ... what I consider one of the main characteristics of the symbolic
> acts: they never belong to a known and pre-established repertoire
> of gestures and customs, but are invented for the occasion. The
> prophet is his own author of the script; no script is provided by the
> culture in which he works. He is an imaginative and creative
> performer rather than the magician who relies on traditional
> rituals others cannot or do not dare to use. The prophetic acts
> belong to the history of teaching aids and provocative street theater
> rather than to the phenomenology of magic.

This is strong on assertion but weak on providing supportive
evidence for the analysis. Perhaps the Ezekiel material is easier to
place in a social context (cf. Ezek. 24.15-27; 33.30-33) than the
Jeremiah stories, but neither book is as accessible to our understanding
as Lang's optimistic interpretations would seem to imply. If a
prophet had invented his own script without reference to the social
culture of the day, the actions would have been incomprehensible
without a shared set of concepts. Lang's analysis fails to understand
how cultures work and how performers and audience share a
framework of reference which permits communication in the first
place. Further problems arise in the book of Jeremiah because of the
nature of the literature and the lack of explanatory clarification of
what is being done and how *that* should be understood (e.g. 13.1-7, 8-
11; 25.15-17). Not all the stories are as difficult as these; some are
only ambiguous in their specifications: in 27, for example, did
Jeremiah make yoke-bars *and wear them* in public or did he *send
them* to the neighbouring states?The general import of many of the
acts is clear: the destruction of the nation is the message conveyed by
most of them, so they are variations on the preached word (which so
often accompanies the action). In some cases the destruction of the
enemy is the point of the action (e.g. 32.15, 42-44; 51.59-64), though
in the purchasing of the field in Anathoth only future restoration is
referred to, and the collapse of Babylonian power is merely implicit
in the text. The magic of 51.59-64 has no such implicit message, but
proclaims by actions, words, and gestures the drowning of the great
enemy.

4. Jeremiah the writer

Prophets are speakers; and prophecy is an oral phenomenon. But we only know their work in written forms, so we deal with prophecy in a transformed mode. Writing is seldom posited of prophets, though temple prophets in ancient Mari were associated with writing, and the few references to scribal activities are indicative of its rarity in the traditions (e.g. Isa. 8.1; 30.8; Hab. 2.2; 2 Chron. 21.12). In the book of Jeremiah there are a number of allusions to Jeremiah as a writer of his own work: in 29.1 he writes a letter to the exiles in Babylon (29.24-32 implies an exchange of correspondence); signs a deed in 32.10; writes a book of oracles in 30.2 (contained in 30-31); writes another book of (evil) oracles, this time against Babylon, in 51.60 (containing 50-51? cf. the book referred to in 25.13). So Jeremiah is a frequently published author according to these references! Of course, writing is the great means of communicating at a distance (whether spatial as in 29.1; 51.61 or temporal as in 30.3; Isa. 30.8), and, in a period when various communities of Jews lived in Babylon and Egypt, sets up a network of communications between different groups in diverse locations. Thus in a sense Jeremiah's writing activities may be regarded as another symbolic action as well as reflecting a period when prophetic utterances were being committed to writing. They may also be viewed as a further level in the presentation of Jeremiah *the prophet* who commands the communities no matter where they are: he writes to Babylon (29), he preaches in Egypt (44), but always he is the creative authority who embodies the values and ideology of the producers of the written tradition of Jeremiah.

In 36.1-3 Jeremiah is commanded *to write* on a scroll all the divine words preached by him over the previous twenty-three years. This piece has obvious connections with 25.1-7 where the twenty-three years of preaching are reflected on in a piece of prose, and with 1.2-3 where dates are given which include the same starting-point. But 36 is a very distinctive narrative in the book of Jeremiah, and part of its distinctiveness is conveyed by the fact that *Jeremiah does not write the scroll*! The great writer of books and letters in the tradition here summons Baruch ('the scribe' v. 32) to do his writing for him and dictates to him the scroll of his past speeches. Why should Jeremiah the writer require a scribe on this occasion? As the story unfolds it becomes apparent that Jeremiah no longer has access to the temple (is this before or after 35?), so what he really needs is someone to read his scroll for him. Such restricted access to the temple would not necessitate obtaining a scribe: only finding a reader of the scroll would be required for such a task (cf. Seraiah, the brother of Baruch, in 51.59-64 as the delegated *reader* of Jeremiah's book for Babylon). So the introduction of Baruch in this narrative may indicate that something else is going on in the tradition at this point. What that may have been we do not know. Clearly Jeremiah does not need a writer because on all other occasions he writes his own material. Many scholars regard Baruch as Jeremiah's biographer as well as his amanuensis, but there is absolutely no evidence for this view in the text of 36 (or anywhere else in the book!). It should be noted that in 36.8 Baruch carries out Jeremiah's instructions about reading the scroll in the temple (that is, he reads the scroll in the temple), whereas in vv. 9-26 the story is told in a very different way involving three readings of the scroll, though not all by Baruch!

Given the unusualness of prophets writing their own words and the frequency with which the book of Jeremiah represents Jeremiah (or Baruch!) as writing, what may be said about the figure of Jeremiah as writer? Unless the prophetic books began to be written down in the exilic period it is unlikely that Jeremiah wrote his own book. The book of Ezekiel, which is set roughly in the same period as that of Jeremiah, does not represent Ezekiel as writing things, so the book of Jeremiah is peculiar in this respect. Such unique representations are not easily accounted for because there are no comparative data to work with. This means that we cannot explain why so much emphasis is put on writing in the Jeremiah tradition, other than for the reason of communicating at a distance. Speculation is permissible here. Perhaps at the time when the traditions were being written down and assembled into something vaguely like what we know as the book of Jeremiah glimpses of the processes involved were incorporated into the text. Or it may have been the case that the book of Jeremiah reflects the period when the prophetic traditions were being transformed into written documents. The scribal schools may have played an important part in the production of the book of Jeremiah, and the representation of Baruch in 36 may be a scribal self-portrait. Or the book of Jeremiah may have been regarded as a congeries of small books joined together to make the larger book that we know (LXX and MT indicate different sizes of books, and these may reflect developmental stages of the book's growth). This is all speculative because we know *absolutely nothing* about how such books came into existence. Many scholars prefer to work with the hypothesis that followers of prophets wrote down their words or that the deuteronomists contributed greatly to the construction of Jeremiah. Others (e.g. Holladay, Lundbom) favour the belief that Jeremiah, with Baruch, wrote his own work, arranged and edited it. There is no evidence for such beliefs. All we may do is recognize the figure of Jeremiah in the book as a writer and ponder what that may signify.

5. Jeremiah the representative

A less obvious reading of the book is the view that at certain points in the story Jeremiah takes on the role of spokesman for and representative of city and community. This is less obvious as an interpretation of the text because it depends on making a number of questionable judgments about both the meaning of the text and the application to it of certain principles derived from bits of texts. The poems of lament which speak out the anguish of the community/city (e.g. 4.19-21; 8.18-9.1; 10.19-20; cf. 30.12-16) are not directly attributed to Jeremiah in the text, but 1.1 is made by exegetes to apply to every statement in the book. Where there is mourning the voices are invariably female ones (e.g. 9.17-19, 20-22; 31.15); hence it is easy to transfer that voice in these poems to city or community (cf. Lam. 1.1-3). This female voice resonates in a number of the poems in the book, and we may understand the laments to be the voice of mother Jerusalem bemoaning the loss of her children (10.20; 31.15). But who actually speaks *as* Jerusalem? The feminine metaphors of the city and land reflect their gender in the Hebrew language, but the speaker as representative of city and land need not be a woman for this convention to work. The identity of the speaker is not important, whether he be priest, cult prophet, anonymous poet or someone else. The poems are what count, and they express shock and mourning caused by the devastations of the time. The question whether the poet should be viewed as a 'female impersonator' (Kaiser) or simply as the mouthpiece for conventional laments over the fallen city is hardly very important, though many of the images are drawn from real women's experiences of war and invasion. In time of war the mothers lament the destruction of their children and their young men (9.21).

Many writers make Jeremiah the spokesman of the community's pain and suffering and even treat him as the representative of the people. Many of these laments consequently lose much of their force and reference by becoming expressions of Jeremiah's own feelings (cf. Berridge, Bright, Holladay, Polk on, e.g. 4.19-21 for this loss of meaning). This kind of current interpretation leads to a decided misapplication of texts which renders the laments invisible as expressions of communal loss and transforms them into statements by Jeremiah about his own inner moods. A similar process can also be seen in the treatment of the laments in 11-20 which removes them from the sphere of righteous-versus-wicked complaints and makes them private expressions of grief and anger by Jeremiah about himself. These misprisions of the text are due to faulty interpretative procedures and are in no sense caused by the editing policies behind the texts. The language of the laments appears in 30.12-16 where there can be no mistaking its referent as the city-community, so when we encounter this kind of language in 4-10 or 11-20 the most likely area of meaning for it must be as expressions of the community's pain (differentiated, perhaps, in 11-20 in terms of the suffering of the righteous and the oppression of the wicked). If we make Jeremiah the speaker of these poems (not a necessary move) then we must see him as the representative of the community giving expression to the city-people's pain and loss rather than as making private comments about his own situation. That is the logic of treating Jeremiah in the book as representative.

This reading of the text clearly creates a cluster of problems, for if Jeremiah is understood as being the people's representative, how can he also be viewed as the opponent of the community? Many of the poems are too critical of the nation to be regarded as expressions of the people's representative. This is essentially a problem of the way we read the text: it is unnecessary to insist that every poem or narrative must be an expression of Jeremiah's just because at some stage in the book's history it has been edited that way and has had 1.1-3 affixed to it. A consistent line of interpretation can be argued for in terms of Jeremiah, the prophet to the nations, as the community's representative and speaker against the foreign nations. This would link with his location in the temple and give force to Reventlow's arguments that he is a cult prophet who represents the people before Yahweh in the cult. It would, however, conflict with the poems which attack the people and also the cultic harangues in 2–4, because these are so much in opposition to the community that attributing them to a representative would make no sense at all. What is being argued here is simply this: a case can be made out for Jeremiah as representative from *parts* of the text, but most definitely not from *all* the text taken together. Among exegetes who see elements of his representativeness in the text there is often a deeply inconsistent reading of the poems of opposition which fails to see in the hostility and divisiveness of the speaker a refusal to be identified with the whole community. 'Jeremiah as representative' is only *one* strand in the book and not a comprehensive understanding of the tradition which can be applied throughout it.

In keeping with the tone of this book it is important to scrutinize the language of the text in order to harvest every nuance of language and metaphor. Much of the secondary literature does not pay sufficient attention to the linguistic nuances of the poems which bemoan the fate of the community, because of its concern to attribute everything to Jeremiah as spokesman. This elevation of one strand of the tradition to a meta-semantic level distorts the interpretation of all the other strands and collapses under the weight of its own incoherencies. In isolating the motif of Jeremiah the representative (a motif highlighted by the LXX's attribution of the book of Lamentations to Jeremiah) it is imperative that we recognize the subsequent shifts which must take place in our treatment of the other motifs. The one who prays for the destruction of the people (e.g. 6.11; 11.20; 12.3b; 15.15; 17.18; 18.21-23; 20.12) can hardly *also* be the one who stands as their representative before Yahweh (e.g. 10.23-25; 42.1-6; cf. 18.20?). The preacher of repentance motif adds to the difficulty of determining how all these various strands are to be turned into a coherent and consistent depiction of Jeremiah. Perhaps we should not be trying to make everything in the book contribute to an identikit picture of an imagined Jeremiah!

6. Jeremiah and Baruch

At certain points in the book Jeremiah is represented as associating with one Baruch the son of Neriah (32.12-14; 36.4-32; 43.3-6; 45.1-2). These four pieces are by no means uniform narratives, and three of them only permit a brief glimpse of Baruch. He is referred to in

32.12-14 without any account given why he should be with Jeremiah (vv. 1-5 belong to the editorial framework and may not be original to the story of the land purchase). He takes charge of the signed deeds and conceals them in an earthenware jar. Whether he was a member of Jeremiah's entourage or just one of the Jews who were in the guardhouse at the time is unknown. The book of Jeremiah is rather parsimonious with information about either Jeremiah or Baruch. In 43.3-6 he is associated with Jeremiah, accused of being in a conspiracy against the community, and taken down to Egypt with Jeremiah (as companion?). He thereafter disappears from view. His only serious role is in 36 where he writes at Jeremiah's dictation the scroll of his speeches and so earns the epithet 'the scribe' (36.32). A brief oracle in 45 is linked to 36 by means of the editorial framework and associates a lament of Baruch's with the occasion of the scroll-writing episode. So the amount of material in the book on Baruch is not very great.

An association between a prophet and another person is unique in the collected anthologies constituting the prophetic traditions. Only in the prophetic stories incorporated into the volumes of Kings are there any analogies: there is some contact between Elijah and Elisha in 1 Kgs 19.19-21; 2 Kgs 2.1-15, and in 2 Kgs 4-5 Elisha is represented as having a servant called Gehazi. But what relationship does Jeremiah have with Baruch? In 32 he is among the witnesses to the property transaction, in 36 he acts as a secretary on one/two(!) occasion(s), in 43 he is possibly a companion or associate, and in 45 he is made the recipient of a divine word. Nothing in this short list is consistent or clear enough to suggest a definite association between the two men. Yet we must take note of the connections between the two because *outside the book of Jeremiah* they are an important pair of companions at two levels. In the extra-biblical literature they constitute a topos (i.e. a commonplace and recurrent motif), the beginnings of which are clearly in the biblical text itself (see the next section below). Also in modern scholarship many writers on the book of Jeremiah regard Baruch as an important figure in the production of the book or, at least, as the writer of parts of it (see Chapters 3, 4 above). These are two very significant levels of development of the pair and, whatever view may be taken of either or both, can hardly be ignored even in an introduction to Jeremiah studies.

I have already pointed out the incoherence of 36 as evidence of the way in which prophetic books were written, and have noted the circularity of the argument which uses 36 as supporting evidence for the interpretation of 36. Even taken as a literal eyewitness account, 36 would tell us virtually nothing about how the book of Jeremiah was written because we do not know which parts of the present book constituted the contents of either of Baruch's scrolls. The assumption that there must be a direct correlation of Baruch's scroll with our book of Jeremiah is audacious but utterly unconfirmable in any sense. There are, furthermore, many features of the narrative in 36 which are stylistically linked to 25.1-14; 26 and to 2 Kings 22; and these common elements should cause us to question the literal reading of 36 *as both history and a reliable account of the origins of the book of Jeremiah*. If we follow the structural analysis of 36 in conjunction with a reading of 26 (i.e. as the end and the beginning of part III), then it is possible to see in the introduction of Baruch as writer of the scroll the procurement of one who could read the scroll (the ability to write implies the capacity to read) *in the absence of the original speaker Jeremiah* To explain that absence (beyond the non-information given in 36.5) requires knowing that the words will be burned at some stage in the proceedings (burned words can be rewritten, burned prophets or scribes cannot be reconstituted!) and that there are symmetrical presences and absences (of kings and prophets) in 36 and 26. It is therefore unnecessary to boost the role of Baruch into Jeremiah's scribe on all other occasions of his setting things down in writing. Since even the editors see no need to rewrite the tradition in terms of Baruch as its transmitter, why should modern exegetes overload 36 with significance? It is sufficient that a few stories in the book associate Jeremiah with Baruch; with time and the use of the same kind of imagination the two will eventually become bosom friends.

7. Jeremiah after Jeremiah

The afterlife of the figure of Jeremiah has been a considerable one. He and Baruch appear as two very lively figures in the extra-biblical literature which extends into the Common era; and the stories told about these two worthies may well raise for us the question of the nature of the material about them in the biblical book. No scholars have any difficulty recognizing the *legendary* nature of the stories of

Jeremiah and/or Baruch in the apocryphal and pseudepigraphal
literature, and it is therefore only proper and logical to ask the
obvious question: 'why should not the stories about Jeremiah and
Baruch in the Bible also be viewed as legendary in nature?'. To this
question there is no good answer except the acknowledgment that
both sets of stories display *the same kind* of imaginative and creative
storytelling qualities. To accord theological privilege to the biblical
stories is regarded as professionally illegitmate by heremeneuts and
exegetes, and will not be indulged in here. We should perhaps
recognize the common world inhabited by the Bible, the Apocrypha,
the Pseudepigrapha, the New Testament, and other writings of the
second temple period. All the prophets have an afterlife outside the
biblical books, though it may be the case that Jeremiah and Baruch
are particularly well-favoured in being the topos of so many
stories.

The book of Jeremiah contains no information about the girth or
death of Jeremiah: it is not biography in that sense at all. Stories of
his death appear in the extra-biblical literature, but there is no
consistent account of it. In *The Lives of the Prophets* he dies in Egypt
stoned by the people, whereas in the *Paraleipomena* of Jeremiah he is
stoned by the people after returning from Babylon with the exiles—
in this account his stoning comes about as a result of his having a
Christian vision which naturally upset the Jews in the temple! In this
literature he exercises a ministry in Egypt, in Babylon, and also back
in Palestine after the exile. The canonical book abandons him in
Egypt after 44. We may assume that he died there, but the Bible has
no interest in biographical facts about Jeremiah. In the other
literature he does great good to the Egyptians by ridding their land of
monsters and snakes (a kind of Hebrew St Patrick!); in Babylon he
instructs the exiles throughout the exile, and back in Palestine he
imposes marriage rules on the people similar to those written about
in the books of Ezra and Nehemiah. He is also referred to as
'Jeremiah the priest' (*Paraleipomena* 5.18); and, at times, the
relationship between him and Baruch is that of father to son
(metaphorical and religious rather than biological!). As a priest he
takes control of the sacred temple vessels and makes sure that they
are well hidden during the period of Babylonian hegemony in
Palestine (cf. 2 Macc. 2.1-8; *Lives of the Prophets* 2.11-19). The
stories about Jeremiah's protection of the sacred vessels contrast

strikingly with the passing references to them in the biblical tradition (27.18-22; much of which is lacking in the LXX: 28.3, 6) and show a creative freedom on the part of the extra-biblical writers which is at odds with some theories of preternatural 'respect for scripture' in the ancient Jewish world! What all the literature has in common is a set of topoi provided by or present in the biblical stories, but there are no requirements of consistency or lack of contradiction. The stories have a life of their own and develop a world of storytelling shared with the Bible in which Jeremiah and Baruch live on to have many adventures together.

In *The Syriac Apocalypse of Baruch* (*2 Baruch*) the action tends to be determined by Baruch rather than by Jeremiah: Baruch speaks against Babylon, he survives the exile so that he is available to explain the disaster to other cities, and he it is who communicates by letter with the other tribes. As a scribe it is only natural that he should become a seer credited with producing apocalypses of his own; and in circles where apocalypses flourished it is Baruch who is the hero. Perhaps the strands in the book of Jeremiah where he appears are indicative already of a tendency for the scribe to displace the prophet (a feature of apocalpyse-writing!): he writes Jeremiah's scroll and reads it out in the temple, he takes control of the jar containing the deeds of Jeremiah's land purchase, and in 43.3 he is accused of being the brains behind Jeremiah's conspiracy to have the Babylonians destroy the Judean community.

The story of Jeremiah and Baruch outside the canon of scripture recognized by Jews and Protestants could be told at much greater length, but what has been given here should be sufficient to indicate the fact that tales about these two companions are very much a feature of Greco-Roman times. Elsewhere one may note the influence of the book of Jeremiah on Jewish and Christian Literature: for example, the 'seventy years' motif of 25.11-12; 29.10 (capable of many interpretations, cf. Carroll, 493-95) appears in Zech. 1.12; 7.5; Dan. 9.2; 2 Chron. 36.21 (the latter two references cite Jeremiah as their source for it), though some have argued that the book of Jeremiah took it from Zechariah (e.g. Duhm, 202). The influence of the book on the New Testament is considerable (typified by Mt. 16.16?), especially the pericope about the new covenant in 31.31-34 (cited in Heb. 8.8-13; 10.15-17; alluded to in some versions of Mt. 26.28; Mk 14.24; Lk. 22.20?). Baruch, however, does not appear to have had any effect on the writers of the New Testament.

Jeremiah's association with the lament mode of expression and his reputation as the author of the book of Lamentations have given rise to the word 'jeremiad' meaning 'a long mournful lamentation or complaining diatribe'. In later legends he has even been credited with taking the Blarney Stone to Ireland and recently has been made the figure behind the creation of eight books of the Bible (he is identified by Friedman as the Deuteronomist who produced Deuteronomy, the Deuteronomistic History, and his own book of Jeremiah). He is identified as the first Jew, the supreme individualist in the Hebrew Bible, the great champion of private religion, a mystic and a saint. It should be obvious to the reader that modern scholars have a tendency to lose all sense of proportion when reading the book of Jeremiah.

Further Reading

The citation is from J. Steinmann, *Le prophète Jérémie: Sa vie, son œuvre et son temps* (Lectio divina 9), Paris: Editions du Cerf, 1952, 296.

For the Egyptian images of pre-conception divine knowledge see W. Beyerlin (ed.), *Near Eastern Texts relating to the Old Testament* (OTL), London: SCM Press, 1978, 27-30. A.R. Johnson, *The Cultic Prophet in Ancient Israel*, 2nd edn, Cardiff: University of Wales Press, 1962 is a good introduction to the concept of the cult prophet; Reventlow, *Liturgie*, gives the fullest account of the arguments for viewing Jeremiah as a cult prophet.

The citation of Lang is from his article 'Street Theater', in Lust, 305 (details in Chapter 6 'Further Reading'). The transformations brought about by writing may be studied in J. Goody, *The Logic of Writing and the Organization of Society* (Studies in Literacy, Family, Culture and the State), Cambridge: Cambridge University Press, 1986; W.J. Ong, *Orality and Literacy: The Technologizing of the Word* (New Accents), London: Methuen, 1982.

On the female voice of the lament see B.B. Kaiser, 'Poet as "Female Impersonator": The Image of Daughter Zion as Speaker in Biblical Poems of Suffering', *The Journal of Religion* 67, 1987, 164-82. On representativeness and identity in the laments see Berridge, *Prophet* and Polk, *Prophetic Persona* for more traditionalist readings of the text (despite the sophistications of their approaches).

The different strands of Baruch material are well dealt with in Wanke, *Untersuchungen*.

The extra-biblical books featuring Jeremiah and Baruch may be found in J.H. Charlesworth (ed.), *The Old Testament Pseudepigrapha*, London: Darton, Longman & Todd, London, vol. I, 1983; vol. II, 1985; M. de Jonge (ed.), *Outside the Old Testament*, Cambridge: Cambridge University Press, 1986; H.F.D. Sparks (ed.), *The Apocryphal Old Testament*, Oxford: Clarendon Press, 1984.

8

THE
THEOPOLITICS
OF THE BOOK

All interpretations originate in politics, which is to say, in
values.

> E.D. Hirsch, Jr

This book will argue the priority of the political interpretation of
literary texts. It conceives of *the political perspective* not as some
supplementary method, not as an optional auxiliary to other
interpretive methods current today—the psychoanalytic or the
myth-critical, the stylistic, the ethical, the structural—but rather *as
the absolute horizon of all reading and all interpretation.*

> Fredric Jameson

TRADITIONAL AND CONVENTIONAL readings of the book of
Jeremiah see in it the struggle of the prophet during the period
627-587 to persuade the people and their leaders of the need to
change religious and political policies in order to avoid imminent
destruction. Even that summary of the standard interpretations of
Jeremiah highlights the political nature of the book. The colophon of
1.1-3 sets the preaching of Jeremiah in the closing decades of the
existence of the state of Judah (cf. the setting of the book of Isaiah
during the Assyrian crisis in Isa. 1.1 and of the book of Ezekiel during
the Babylonian exile in Ezek. 1.1-3), as the kingdom crumbles under
the pressures of internal and external forces. Whatever the historical
status granted to 1.1-3, no approach to the book will deny its
profoundly political and polemical nature nor fail to recognize the
competing and conflicting voices to be heard in the tradition. What
these different voices may represent is always debatable because the
text has been highly edited over a long period of time and conceals
much more than it reveals. If, however, we read the book as the
product of *one* voice and confine that voice to the period defined by
1.1-3 we shall have grave difficulties in understanding the book at all.

Its diversities, its contrary and contradictory voices, and its ragbag qualities will all be lost to a procrustean approach which will render the book fit only for pious consumption. It is important therefore that we make due allowance for the sheer untidiness of the book and for the multiplicity of viewpoints which constitute it. No approach to or interpretation of Jeremiah which is not itself untidy, diverse, polemical and multiple will have any chance of taking the measure of this sprawling, angry biblical volume.

The political is primary! Modern distinctions between the political and the religious are virtually unknown in the ancient world in that the sharp differentiations between the two spheres are not to be found there. In the Hebrew Bible Yahweh's temple and the royal palace are part of the same complex of buildings and the king is both son of David and son of Yahweh (cf. Pss. 2.7; 45.6). Thus to criticize the king is to make both a political and a religious statement at the same time. Outside Jerusalem rather different views about kingship may have existed, and these would have been equally hostile to the temple complex as well (cf. Mic. 1-3 for a scathing critique of the whole Jerusalem culture). The ideologies of support and opposition in the Bible are expressed in religious language because this is how ancient politics was played. So when we read such harangues against religious practices as appear in Jer. 2-3 or contemplate the critique of temple worship (6.20; 7.1-15; 11.15; 19.3-13) we should not naively imagine that here we have the voice of 'true' religion attacking the practitioners of 'false' religion (cf. the tone of 44), but should recognize the highly political and partisan nature of the ideology being expressed. The simple reading of the text which refuses interpretation is itself a highly charged political stance which chooses to accept the ideological presuppositions of the writer of the text as if they were a set of *neutral* observations and descriptions of an unmediated reality! Interpretation is necessary because the text itself is already a series of political interpretations and gestures made by various parties in support of ideologies which may not always be apparent at a first reading of the text. So the book of Jeremiah needs to be scrutinized very closely by the reader so that its ideological opacities may become transparent.

2.1-2, 4-5a introduce a lengthy series of oracular fulminations against the families of Israel, but the producers of the book have prefaced 2-3 with a series of prologue elements which focus attention on Jeremiah the prophet to the nations. Set in a period when all the state institutions are collapsing and the kingdoms of the north are gathering against Jerusalem, the writers wish us to contemplate these fateful times from the perspective of a prophet who is divinely appointed over the nations 'to pluck up and to break down, to destroy and to overthrow, to build and to plant' (1.10; cf. 12.14-17; 18.7, 9; 24.6; 31.28, 40; 42.10; 45.4; note how Ben Sira in Ecclus 49.6-7 singles out these activities, following LXX's five terms rather than MT's six, to characterize the work and significance of Jeremiah). The echoes of an Egyptian royal legitimation motif in 1.5 (cf. Isa. 49.2, 5) may (or there again may not!) hint at the presentation of Jeremiah as the true authority in the land rather than the inept kings whose policies brought about the destruction of Jerusalem and Judah. Certainly the book of Jeremiah is dominated by the ideology of the divine word mediated by the prophet (transformed into writing in a number of instances, e.g. 36; 29.1, 4-7; 30-31; 51.59-64); and this ideology criticizes every institutional authority in the land (kings, prophets, priests, wise men). Absolutely no authority or value in Judean society is exempted from the critique of this word, so the figure of Jeremiah towers over everything in the culture. Jeremiah is the means whereby this ideology of the word opposes everything, and he proclaims this word throughout the lands of Judah and Egypt. By turning it into writing he also communicates it to the land of Babylon. Nowhere is exempt from hearing it. The word is king! The word is the true and only authority which determines the structures of society and all opposition to it is futile. This reading of the book of Jeremiah shows this word to be a theopolitical concept. It is mediated by the prophet and represents the various values behind the editing of the text. Such a word-ideology is not an uncreated entity of an absolute kind, but the construction of the groups whose values are embodied in the text. It flourishes in a time of breakdown and disintegration when the social institutions have fallen apart and all authority figures have been confounded. It also has a life of its own which permits it to function within any given social structure without being tied to temple or court. Wherever the people gather, be it in the ruins of Jerusalem or the sandy wastes of the desert or the upper reaches of the Nile or beside the irrigation canals of Babylon, the word may be preached or read and teaching authorities thrive.

The almost complete absence of the king in 2-20 (passing

reference is made of the kings in 3.6; 4.9; 8.1; 13.18; 15.4; 17.20, 25; 19.4, 13) in contrast to the role of the king in the narratives and editorial framework of 21-25, 26-29, 33-39, 45 is perhaps indicative of the development of the poems in a society lacking kings (Yahweh is the king in 8.19; 10.7, 10). Kingship as such is not opposed in the cycle of 21.11-23.6, but the cycle itself may have been added as part of the appendix to 2-20 because the collection lacked a serious treatment of kingship. The narratives, on the other hand, present Jeremiah in confrontation or conversation with individual kings (26-45) and make the king's response determinative of the nation's fate (36.20-32; 37.1-2; cf. 15.4; 52.1-3). This is a very different approach from the critiques of society in 2-20 and the attacks on the prophets in 23.9-40 (cf. 27-29) and indicates the presence of different voices in the tradition. One dominant storyline in the book is that of Jeremiah in conjunction with the king (mainly Zedekiah, but Jehoiakim is glimpsed in the editing of 26.1, 20-23, and Jeremiah is absent in 36.20-26). The encounter is told again and again as variations on a single theme (21/34/37/38) and must represent an editorial conviction that a key to understanding the destruction of Jerusalem was Zedekiah's failure to respond to Jeremiah. That is to tell the story of the catastrophe from the perspective of the prophetic word and lacks all subtlety of political reflection. But it does underline the nature of the theopolitics of the book's producers: Babylon established its hegemony over Judah because king Zedekiah failed to yield to the persuasion of Jeremiah the prophet. Such an assessment of the last decade of Judean statehood is a profoundly lopsided one, but that is how the stories of Jeremiah and Zedekiah read the situation.

There is, of course, no single line of interpretation present in the book of Jeremiah. Too many different ideologies clash within it for that to be the case. Even on the subject of the kings there is no simple viewpoint exclusively employed: for example, the enormous hostility displayed towards king Coniah (variously Jehoiachin or Jeconiah) in 22.24-30, which is almost inexplicable in view of the brevity of his reign (note how his reign is glossed over in 37.1), is very different from the attitude shown towards him by the deuteronomistic epilogue to Jeremiah in 52.31-34. Acute antagonism appears to be a constant in the treatment of king Jehoiakim: the editing of 22.18a makes vv. 13-19 seem to refer to him, 26.20-23 presents him as vicious, and 36.20-26 is not favourable towards him. But he is not a significant figure in the tradition, and only part of 36 is directly concerned with him. A few passing references to kings Josiah and Shallum (22.11) show them to be of no significance in the book: an insignificance easily overlooked by commentators' tendency to overread 1.2; 3.6; 22.15b-16; 25.3; 36.2! In 34.4-5; 38.17, 24-28 there is a bond of sympathy displayed between Jeremiah and Zedekiah which runs counter to any theory of hostility towards the kings as a principle behind the editing of the book. It also illustrates well the point being made about the lack of a single line of theopolitical evaluation of kings and kingship. At various points in the prose of the tradition kingship is valued positively (e.g. 22.1-4; cf. 17.19-25; also 23.5-6=33.14-16; 33.17-26) and a few traces survive in the book of hopes for future kings. Such positive appreciations of kingship are too minor an element in the book to be other than peripheral; and, the narratives apart, the monarchy must be viewed as an irrelevance of the past, unimportant in comparison to the prophetically mediated divine word.

Ironically the book which so lauds the prophetic word is also the very book which most consistently denounces the prophets. Jeremiah excepted—and here we must remember the differences between the first and second editions' uses of the epithet 'the prophet'—no prophet is presented in a positive light (Uriah of Kiriath-jearim in 26.20-23 is only mentioned parenthetically as it were) and this is a dominant feature of the tradition. In 2-20 dismissals of the prophets tend to be perfunctory (e.g. 2.8, 26b; 4.9; 5.31; 6.12=8.10), though 14.13-16 summarizes the arguments used elsewhere to condemn them. Two cycles of material are devoted to attacking the prophets comprehensively both in general terms (23.9-40) and over specific matters about Babylonian hegemony (27-29). In 23.9-40 Jeremiah does not appear at all, and the cycle is not edited as a dismissal of the prophets in favour of Jeremiah. On the contrary, *all* the prophets are condemned and blamed for spreading godlessness throughout the land (vv. 14-15). The techniques used by them are also denounced (vv. 25-32), with unspecific hints about the word being in sharp contrast to prophetic media of revelation (cf. vv. 28-29). Judging the cycle as it stands leaves the impression that prophets *per se* are the target of these pieces, and there are some indications that the prophets are being held responsible for the destruction of the city (cf. v. 39). The cycle is by no means all of a piece, and it is impossible to date anything in it. Whether it should be regarded as reflecting pre-destruction polemics against the prophets of Jerusalem or exilic and post-exilic controversies against groups of prophets cannot now be established. Most commentators favour reading the cycle as Jeremiah's attack on the prophets who misled the community before the catastrophe, but nothing in the text justifies this reading of it. It is therefore like very much other material in the book which cannot be dated on internal grounds nor applied to any specific occasions (for example, a reading of the poems in 2–20 will not furnish evidence to distinguish which ones may apply to the invasion of 597 and which to that of 587: the poetry is remarkably imprecise in concrete references!).

In 27–29 the editorial framework provides a setting for the narratives and clearly presents the material as the work of the prophet (MT) Jeremiah against the community's prophets in Jerusalem (or in Babylon). It is therefore a very different cycle from that in 23.9-40. The cycle also addresses one specific issue: submission to Babylonian hegemony, whether in Palestine or in Babylonia itself. Jeremiah is represented as the spokesman for the pro-Babylonian viewpoint and all opponents of that political party are condemned out of hand. The story of Hananiah and Jeremiah in 28 is an exemplification of this principle. Now whether Jeremiah should be regarded as a traitor to his own people (cf. 38.4), a quisling or an agent of a foreign power, is not clear from the text; and the kind of information afforded by the book is not of the type which would allow any reader to be able to determine the issue satisfactorily. The representation of Babylon in 27–29 is in striking contrast to its presentation in 50–51, but both cycles of texts reflect very opposing views and evaluations of the empire. As Jeremiah is made the progenitor of both sets of opinions it is probably wiser to regard Jeremiah's association with such opposing viewpoints as rather an editorial creation than a reflection of a genuine historical position adopted by Jeremiah. But the political nature of the cycle cannot be missed by the intelligent reader, and some account is required of the contrary and contradictory attitudes to Babylon in the book of Jeremiah.

27–29 unmistakably make Jeremiah the locus of correct ideology, and all prophetic activity which does not agree with him is false. Movements of support for the king in exile, opposition to the

Babylonians and beliefs in Jerusalem as the centre of divine activity are all dismissed in favour of Babylonian hegemony and the permanence of life in Babylon for the exiles of 597. Any prophet identified with an alternative viewpoint is denounced throughout 27–29. Thus Jeremiah is brought into a pro-Babylonian polemic against Jerusalem, the temple cult, and the prophets. As spokesman for the Babylonian Jews (contrast 32.6-15; 42.7-12) he is not politically neutral but very much a partisan voice. Now in this area it is very easy for exegetes naively to assume that the voice of Jeremiah simply represents the divine word untouched by human intrigue and politics. The divine word as spoken by human beings is always some *particular* individual's word and reflects the cultural, social, and historical context of that person's existence. There are no *unmediated* divine words which bypass the consciousness or circumstances of the human speaker; all such words are the products of human culture and tend to reinforce the values of the people speaking them. 27–29 attempt to put the case for the new Jewish communities in Babylonia which require ideological justification over against the Jewish communities of Palestine and Egypt. Much in the book of Jeremiah denounces the people who live in Jerusalem–Judah and in Egypt, so to find a cycle which legitimates the Jewish deportees in Babylon (cf. 24.4-7, 8-10) raises the question whether the book might not, in some way or other, be propaganda for the Babylonian Jews (cf. 29.10-14, 16-19). Too many disparate voices are heard in the book for it to be reduced to a single explanation of propaganda for one group, but that element is at the heart of parts of the book and reflects how deeply political it is.

Nebuchadrezzar, the emperor of Babylon, is represented in 27.6 and throughout the cycle as Yahweh's servant (also in 25.9; LXX lacks 'servant' in 25.9 and is somewhat different in 27.6). As Yahweh's devotee, emissary or vassal (the word for 'servant' in the Hebrew Bible is a term with a wide range of meanings) Nebuchadrezzar is a very important person who cannot be opposed, because to oppose him would be to oppose Yahweh! When Hananiah bravely opposes him in 28 he is struck down for uttering *rebellion against Yahweh* (v. 17; cf. 29.32). Thus opposition to Babylon is equivalent to blasphemy, and submission to Babylon is loyalty to Yahweh. Here the ideology of the Babylonian group is unmistakable. Conformity to Babylonian values and obedience to Nebuchadrezzar's dictates are to be equated with serving Yahweh, and any opposition to Babylonian terms is denounced as false and as being against Yahweh. Such conformity to the politics of the empire makes a striking contrast with the polemics in 2–3 which appear to condemn conformity to the religio-political values of the neighbouring states! Also it is completely contradictory to the denunciations of Babylon in the OAN of 50–51, especially to the representation of Nebuchadrezzar as a dragon (51.34). There is, of course, no single viewpoint in the book of Jeremiah, and nowhere is this truth more obvious than in the representations of Nebuchadrezzar as Yahweh's servant and also as the dragon which has swallowed Zion. There is also a perfectly good explanation of these contradictory evaluations of Babylon: the conformistic and sycophantic attitudes towards the empire stem from groups which must learn to live in peace (cf. 29.7) in and with the empire; the anti-Babylonian attitudes come from those who lived under the empire's heel and eked out a bare subsistence in lands devastated by the military hordes of Babylon. Party politics is the key to understanding these features of the book of Jeremiah.

Partisan politics dominate the book and may be used to explain the various contrary sections. It is difficult, however, to be more specific here because the cycles are not easily located in time or place. 27–29 could represent the placing in Jeremiah's mouth of words legitimating the settled existence of Jews in Babylon and encouraging them to develop normal patterns of life there reflecting the permanence of deportation. There are elements in the book which hint at a return from Babylon (24.4-7; 29.10-14; cf. the more general diaspora return of 31.7-9, 11-12, 16), but these have not entirely obscured the theme of the permanence of exile in Babylon. We know from history (i.e. hindsight!) that the Jewish communities in Babylonia were a permanent feature of the next *two-and-one-half millennia* of Jewish existence, so we also know that hopes about a return to Palestine were mythic or aspirational at best (a few descendants of the original exiles may have returned permanently, but there is no evidence of a wide-scale return). So do the elements preaching a return represent forces at work in Babylon or in Jerusalem? 29 generally attacks voices in Babylon encouraging a return, but the fragments of a return motif may belong with whatever movements are to be associated with the books of Ezra and Nehemiah (the historicity of the person of Ezra remains a controversial issue in modern biblical studies) which may reflect political forces operating in Jerusalem in the fifth and fourth centuries BCE. The denunciations of the Jerusalem community which are so prominent in 2–20 and the dismissal of the Jewish communities in Egypt (44; cf. 42.13-22) allow the material legitimating the Babylonian Jews to emerge as a claim on their behalf to domination of Jerusalem in the second temple period. Now whether this impression is one intended by the editors or just a modern reading of the text must remain an open question because we cannot pin the text down to the kind of specifics which would answer the question one way or the other. Such a theopolitical reading of the book of Jeremiah makes connections between it and the tales told in the books of Ezra and Nehemiah (there are obvious connections between 17.19-27 and Neh. 13.15-18), but without being able to clarify the situation entirely to our own satisfaction.

The differentiation between the exiles who were deported in 597 and those who lived on in Jerusalem until 587, whatever their eventual fate, should be noted as a minor feature of the book (e.g. 24.4-7, 8-10; 29.10-14, 16-19; in striking contrast is 42.1-12!). Such differentiations are very important elements in Jeremiah (note the gradations of 21.6-10) and may have theopolitical factors behind them. In the Jerusalem of the second temple era there must have been many different voices seeking power and representation in order to control the destinies of the city now reduced to provincial status in an unimportant part of the Persian empire. The sharp distinction made in the book between those who were deported in 597 and those exiled in 587 may represent a claim to special status in the new community. This claim may have been to the effect that those who could trace (or assert?) their ancestry to those exiles who had gone to Babylon with king Jehoiachin, rather than say with king Zedekiah (though note the invented deportation of king Jehoiakim in 605 according to Dan. 1.1-4) when Jerusalem was destroyed, possessed a pedigree which entitled them to organize the reconstructed Jerusalem. Such identity, where acceptable and assured, would allow them to outrank even those who had remained behind in Palestine throughout the Babylonian period. The dismissal of the natives is incorporated into the anti-Zedekiah material; and wherever the post-597 people went (be it Babylon, Egypt, or somewhere in Palestine) they are condemned (40.7-42.12 belong to very different cycles of material and conflict with the pro-Babylonian deportation motifs).

The argument here is akin to the claims in Great Britain that people who came over with William the Conqueror outrank the native Anglo-Saxon and all subsequent arrivals and so constitute an elite of 'natural' rulers of the land, or, in America, that those who can trace their ancestry to those who came over in *The Mayflower* outrank the native Red Indian and all subsequent waves of immigrants to the country. It is a matter of *Realpolitik* and, however fanciful the argument may be, reflects the kind of hierarchical status-seeking which all communities indulge in as a way of justifying power, position, privilege and status. There are only traces of this kind of politicking in the book of Jeremiah but we should recognize them as an essential part of the theopolitics of the tradition.

Part of the difficulty of reading the book today is the problem of reconciling all these contrary voices as the representations of just one voice. We know that one person cannot assume so many contradictory positions or represent so multiple a set of disparate values, especially when many of these issues belong to a wide spectrum of time and place. In reading the book of Jeremiah as a concatenation of many distinct voices we interpret it as other than the production of one voice. The theopolitics of the book militate against the fictional representation of it as the *single* voice of Jeremiah the prophet. This is very much a result of the modern approach to texts which focuses on the contradictions and difficulties in the Bible and which seeks to explain them in terms of the development of the tradition. However, it is also the product of reading all texts as political statements. Now in reading the book of Jeremiah from a political perspective no injustice is done to the text because the theopolitical nature of the material in Jeremiah is obvious to every reader of the book. The irreconcilability of the different cycles of material in Jeremiah prompts the political analysis of the text as a way of making sense of the book. It should not, however, be assumed that even a theopolitical reading will make it appear tidy and rational. The book remains a palimpsest of many different opinions acquired over the long period of its production. Too many interests and factions have contributed to its construction for it to represent a single viewpoint, not even that of its final editors! To some extent the figure of Jeremiah holds together the conflicting viewoints of the book, but even that construct of a central figure is far less realized than many exegetes imagine. In places Jeremiah disappears altogether (e.g. 40.7–41.18);

elsewhere it is possible to discern Baruch emerging from the depths to displace him (e.g. 43.3; 45.2-5), and frequently the only connection between Jeremiah and the poems is an over-extended use of 1.1-3 by most commentators. So few of the elements constituting the book are datable, and the social background of many of them equally obscure, that the book may represent many and various political movements from the fall of Jerusalem to the Greco-Roman period. As we know little about this period it is extremely hazardous to try to make too firm a connection between the book and its possible historical background. Even the theopolitical approach may assume more knowledge than we are entitled to claim, but if all our interpretations of the text are allowed to coexist with an awareness of our overwhelming ignorance, then the theopolitical reading of the book may also serve a useful purpose.

Further Reading

Citations are from E.D. Hirsch, Jr, 'The Politics of Theories of Interpretation', *Critical Inquiry* 9, 1982, 235 and F. Jameson, *The Political Unconscious: Narrative as a Socially Symbolic Act*, London: Methuen, 1981, 1986 reprint, 17 (emphases added). For the 'refusal of interpretation' approach (though not specifically related to the Bible) see S. Sontag, 'Against Interpretation', in *Against Interpretation and other essays*, London: André Deutsch, 1987, orig. edn, 1967, 3-14. For the 'primacy of interpretation' approach see S.A. Geller, 'Through Windows and Mirrors into the Bible: History, Literature and Language in the Study of Text', in *A Sense of Text: The Art of Language in the Study of Biblical Literature* (Jewish Quarterly Review Supplement), Winona Lake: Eisenbrauns, 1982, 3-40.

On the divine word element in Jeremiah see the salutary remarks of McKane, *Jeremiah*, xcvii-xcix; *idem*, 'Is there a Place for Theology in the Exegesis of the Hebrew Bible?', *Svensk Exegetisk Årsbok* 50, 1985, 7-20.

Garbini, *History & Ideology*, 151-69 states the case against the historicity of Ezra; Smith, *Palestinian Parties*, 90-95 takes a more traditionalist view of Ezra.

Pohlmann, *Studien* posits an 'exile-orientated redaction' of 37-44 which has expanded the original stories. On 24 see W. Brueggemann, 'A Second Reading of Jeremiah after the Dismantling', *Ex Auditu* 1, 1985, 156-68.

The secondary literature on prophetic conflict in Jeremiah is vast as the motif bears on the larger issues of prophetic validation in the Hebrew Bible; see especially

T.W. Overholt, *The Threat of Falsehood: A Study in the Theology of the Book of Jeremiah* (Studies in Biblical Theology: 2nd series 16), London: SCM Press, 1970.

I. Meyer, *Jeremia und die falschen Propheten* (Orbis Biblicus et Orientalis 13), Göttingen: Vandenhoeck & Ruprecht, 1977.

9

SENSES OF
AN ENDING

THE BOOK OF JEREMIAH is unique among all the prophetic books in that it concludes with a chapter from another book! Its closing chapter is made up of 2 Kgs 24.18-25.30, so that the (so-called) Deuteronomistic History and the book of Jeremiah have the same ending. This is a most strange phenomenon in the Bible and requires some explanation. The simplest account of the matter is to suppose that the editors of the History were also the editors of either the book of Jeremiah or an edition of it. A deuteronomistic edition of Jeremiah is argued for by many scholars, so this simple explanation makes good sense. Why the editors should want to use what is essentially the same collection of pieces to conclude two different books must remain unknown. Perhaps they wanted to indicate the shared editorship or common concern of the two traditions. A similar editorial ploy may be seen in Isa. 36-39 which conclude Isa. 1-39 and which are equivalent to 2 Kgs 18.13-20.19. Only the subsequent addition of Isa. 40-66 to 1-39 has obscured the fact that Isa. 1-35 are also concluded by material from 2 Kings. So perhaps Jeremiah is just a more stark example of a book worked on by the editors of Kings.

Having an additional conclusion to it means that the book of Jeremiah really has *two* endings: The ending it had before the deuteronomistic addition, and the new ending created by the linkage with 2 Kings. As there are also two editions of Jeremiah (MT, LXX) we have in fact *three* different endings or, to be more precise, three *stages* to the ending of the book. Each ending is quite different; and it is worth focusing on all three endings in order to observe the variety of approaches to Jeremiah implicit in them. It should also be noted that 52 lacks any mention of the prophet Jeremiah, as befits the absence of mention by name of any of the prophets from the prophetic anthologies (with the notable exception of Isaiah due to Isa. 36-39=2 Kgs 18.13-20.19) in the Deuteronomistic History. Speculating on the reasons for this absence would entail too lengthy a diversion here and would be subject to all the usual caveats on our ignorance and the sheer lack of reliable information in the Hebrew Bible on such historical matters as prophets and their backgrounds. But the reader of Jeremiah should note carefully that absence of Jeremiah in 52 and the History, whatever reasons may be proffered for it by exegetes.

Both editions of Jeremiah end with 52, so the Greek text reflects a stage in the development of the tradition *after* it had assumed its basic structure of four main blocks of material prefaced by 1 and concluded by 52. The order of the blocks of material was not determined by that stage because both editions reflect alternative placements of the OAN. With those different positionings of part II two very distinctive endings of the story of Jeremiah are available. If we follow the first edition, the story ends with the brief oracle addressed to Baruch in 45 (LXX 51.31-35) and, in essence, the book concludes with the note of survival for at least one individual in a time of evil for all flesh. This note may be regarded as a somewhat positive ending to the tradition so characterized by disaster and evil befalling everyone. In a context of universal disaster Baruch will survive (we might add: and implicitly so will all others who can appropriate the term 'your life as a prize of war', 45.5; cf. 39.19; 38.2; 21.9), and this possibility of survival must be viewed as a benevolent, positive conclusion to a book so dominated by hate, anger, and disaster. Following on from the fierce and almost universal destruction portrayed in 44 the survival of Baruch might be regarded as an earnest of a more positive future.

The second edition ends with the OAN; and its last item before 52 is a report of a narrated action in which Jeremiah writes out (the OAN?) the words of evil against Babylon, has the book taken to Babylon by Seraiah and read out over the city, then cast into the Euphrates so that its drowning symbolizes the permanent drowning of Babylon. Thus does the last note in the story of Jeremiah destroy the evil empire which had itself destroyed so much of the life of the people. Implicit in that destruction is the deliverance of the exiles from Babylon, so that with Babylon's fall comes Zion's rise (the twin motifs belong together in the OAN of 50-51). MT's scribal note in 51.64b observes 'thus far are the words of Jeremiah', that is, the words of Jeremiah are ended. Having done so much throughout the tradition to destroy Jerusalem and to support the Babylonians, in the

OAN Jeremiah performs as a good patriot and speaks the doom of the enemy. And there this version of Jeremiah's story ends. It also, like 45 in the LXX, represents a word of hope about the future. It has a bigger and better hope than 45 because it envisages the destruction of the very power responsible for Judah's pathetic condition during the Babylonian hegemony. With that power overthrown Judah can come back to life, and with the influx of the exiles from Babylon life can flourish again in the land (cf. 31.2-14). The two editions may be contrasted in terms of their endings as a focus on the individual (LXX) and on the community (MT). If LXX is more explicit than MT, what is implicit in the destruction of Babylon should not be missed.

Both endings of the words and activities of Jeremiah are spoiled to some extent by the addition of 52 which does not focus on Jeremiah at all. In terms of the book of Jeremiah 52 goes back to 39, gives further details about the destruction of Jerusalem, and ends on an entirely different note. The obsession of the Deuteronomistic History is with the kings of Judah and especially with their contribution to the fate of Jerusalem. So the fall of Jerusalem is told by the deuteronomistic historians in terms of the wickedness of the Judean kings, hence the initial statement in 52.1-3a. Zedekiah is the guilty party in 52 (how different a representation this is from the friendly interviews between Jeremiah and Zedekiah in 34.1-5; 37–38!) and suffers the full rigours of Nebuchadrezzar's vindictive wrath. Much of the report on the destruction of Jerusalem is taken up with details of the spoliation of the temple and palaces of the city (vv. 17-23). Other details given include the identification of various officials who were executed by Nebuchadrezzar (vv. 24-27) and a register of the numbers deported on three different occasions (vv. 28-30; similar information is not given in 2 Kings 25, but 2 Kgs 24.14, 16 provide numbers for the 597 deportation. Needless to say these numbers differ considerably from Jer. 52.28!). Then the book of Kings/Jeremiah comes to an end with a strange little story about king Jehoiachin (vv. 31-34) and his release from prison (what prison?) after thirty-seven years!

The ending of the book with the touching tale of Jehoiachin's good fortune makes for the third positive ending in Jeremiah. It is traditional to end a book on a relatively happy note (Isa. 66.24 is a notable exception to this principle) and, for all its dyspepsia and violence, the book of Jeremiah in its final form is no exception to this rule. Jehoiachin's fortunate treatment contrasts with the hideous punishments enacted against Zedekiah (vv. 9-11; cf. 39.5-7) and ends the story of the royal sons of David on a happier note than might have been expected from a history so dismal as theirs. The details of the story are simple: Jehoiachin is released c. 660 by Nebuchadrezzar's successor and appointed to a royal pension with the other kings-in-exile until his death. We need not take up space speculating how the king came to be in prison in the first place because information is not available on such matters. There is a hint of bombast in v. 32 where Jehoiachin is placed '*above* the seats of the kings who were with him in Babylon'. Archaeological evidence setting out the Babylonian allocations for Jehoiachin and his family may be regarded as bearing on this story, but offers no information about Jehoiachin *the prisoner* nor singles him out as special.

What may be deduced from 52.31-34? In view of the extreme hostility shown towards Jehoiachin in 22.24-30, this contrary attitude towards him should be noted as an alternative value in the tradition. Perhaps the venomous attack of 22 represents the reverse side of 52, but we know nothing about these political squabbles of ancient times. In the context of 52 Jehoiachin is clearly the legitimate king of Judah, and Zedekiah, as his fate shows only too well, is not. Did then the editors of 52 regard Zedekiah's interregnum period as one when the true Judean king was in exile? Was Hananiah (28.1-4) speaking from such a viewpoint too? May one argue from this ending to the book that hopes still flourished for the return of the king? Was then Jeremiah's opposition to Hananiah in 28 also his rejection of Jehoiachin's status as king? Would that make sense of his friendliness with Zedekiah and his attack on Hananiah? Many questions are raised by 52.31-34 and these should be entertained as ways of reflecting on the text; but answers to them are almost entirely speculative. Technically the History ends the story of the Davidic kings with this story of the final days of the last king of Judah (either as the last *living* king or as the last legitimate king). His days are ended not in dire circumstances, but under relatively pleasant conditions. It is a long way from the sound and fury of David and Solomon, but it is not completely destitute of privilege and comfort. But it is the end of the dynasty! That is one way of reading the significance of 52.31-34. An alternative understanding reads the story as the rehabilitation of Jehoiachin, and so as hinting at an open-ended possibility of survival for the royal house. There the story of the Judean monarchy comes to an end with the release from prison of the last living occupant of the throne. Elsewhere a large family of seven sons is listed for 'Jeconiah the captive' (1 Chron. 3.17-18), but such information is not used here (nor in 2 Chron. 36), so we cannot say that the editors intended their story to be read or heard *as if* the future of the dynasty had been guaranteed by this act of kindness towards the king in exile. We may read the story for what it is worth, but we should be careful not to read too much into it.

This third and final sense of an ending to the book of Jeremiah is in striking contrast to the dominant tenors of the tradition. So many stories of ill-feeling and poems of destruction give to Jeremiah a dark and depressive sense; so much aggression and hatred, cursing and damning, hostility and spite make it an unpleasant book to read. There are, admittedly, a few bright moments in the book when the things which make for being human surface (e.g. 31.2-14), but they are more often swamped by the dominance of anger and pain. So to read as the final entry in this long sorry tale the story of Jehoiachin's release from prison is to glimpse briefly a sunny upland seldom seen in the book of Jeremiah. It is a shaft of sunlight on a darkling plain and it lifts the heart of the reader after a long day's journey through the valley of the shadow.

Further Reading

Consult the commentaries on 2 Kings 25: e.g. J. Gray, *I & II Kings: A Commentary* (OTL) 3rd edn, London: SCM Press, 1977. On the different endings of MT and LXX see P.-M. Bogaert, 'De Baruch à Jérémie: Les deux rédactions conservées du livre de Jérémie', in Bogaert, 168-73.

Useful discussions of the release of Jehoiachin can be found in C.T. Begg, 'The Significance of Jehoiachin's Release: A New Proposal', *JSOT* 36, 1986, 49-56; J.D. Levenson, 'The Last Four Verses of Kings', *JBL* 103, 1984, 153-61; E. Zenger, 'Die deuteronomistische Interpretation der Rehabilitierung Jojachins', *Biblische Zeitschrift* 12, 1968, 16-30.

The problem of Jeremiah's absence in 2 Kings is discussed by Begg, 'A Bible Mystery: the Absence of Jeremiah in the Deuteronomistic History', *Irish Biblical Studies* 7, 1985, 139-64.

Select List of Commentaries

L. Boadt, *Jeremiah 1-25/Jeremiah 26-52, Habakkuk, Zephaniah, Nahum* (Old Testament Message: A Biblical-Theological Commentary 9,10), Wilmington, Delaware: Michael Glazier, 1982. One of the many recent short, pocket-size commentaries available on Jeremiah which will provide the beginner with an introduction to the interpretation of the book.

J. Bright, *Jeremiah: A New Translation with Introduction and Commentary* (Anchor Bible 21), New York: Doubleday & Co., 1965. Not a commentary but a very useful translation with notes and comments by one of the finest American scholars in Jeremiah studies. The lengthy introduction (127 pages) is most valuable.

R.P. Carroll, *Jeremiah: A Commentary* (OTL), London: SCM Press, 1986. The most recent commentary on the whole book, it is sceptical of most traditionalist readings of the text and attempts to interpret the book without assuming anachronistic theological presuppositions about its meaning.

H. Cunliffe-Jones, *The Book of Jeremiah: Introduction and Commentary* (Torch Bible Commentaries), London: SCM Press, 1960. Short and old-fashioned approach to the text, but useful for beginners.

R. Davidson, *Jeremiah I/Jeremiah II with Lamentations* (Daily Study Bible), Edinburgh: Saint Andrew Press, 1983, 1985. More a devotional reading of the text than a proper commentary, but this author brings a wealth of insight to the text which makes his work useful for theological reflection.

R.K. Harrison, *Jeremiah and Lamentations: An Introduction and Commentary* (Tyndale Old Testament Commentaries), London: The Tyndale Press, 1973. A short and rather conservative reading of the text, heavily orientated towards the New Testament.

W.L. Holladay, *Jeremiah 1: A Commentary on the Book of the Prophet Jeremiah Chapters 1-25* (Hermeneia: A Critical and Historical Commentary on the Bible), Philadelphia: Fortress Press, 1986. The first half of what will be the largest commentary on Jeremiah in English when it is completed. A very fine treatment of the text from the historical viewpoint, with a wealth of information on many aspects of the study of Jeremiah. The brevity of its introduction will make the second volume indispensable.

J.P. Hyatt, 'The Book of Jeremiah: Introduction and Exegesis', *The Interpreter's Bible* V, Nashville: Abingdon Press, 1956, 775-1142. Of limited value because so little space remains for exegesis given the penchant of this series for printing two versions of the English text and a section on exposition. Useful as a representation of Hyatt's approach to Jeremiah.

E.A. Leslie, *Jeremiah: Chronologically arranged, translated, and interpreted*, Nashville: Abingdon Press, 1954. A lucid presentation of a conventional reading of Jeremiah which reflects the state of scholarship at the time of its writing.

W. McKane, *A Critical and Exegetical Commentary on Jeremiah*. Vol.I *Introduction and Commentary on Jeremiah I–XXV* (ICC), Edinburgh: T. & T. Clark, 1986. The first volume of a magisterial philological commentary on Jeremiah. Not easy to read, but an invaluable survey of the text, the history of its exegesis, and a concentrated discussion of the modern interpretation of the book. Too technical for the beginner, but should be aspired to by the ambitious student. Its judicious weighing of the evidence and arguments will make it an indispensable commentary.

E.W. Nicholson, *The Book of the Prophet Jeremiah: Chapters 1–25/The Book of the Prophet Jeremiah: Chapters 26–52* (The Cambridge Bible Commentary), Cambridge: Cambridge University Press, 1973, 1975. Based on the New English Bible, this is a characteristically lucid short commentary on Jeremiah. Useful for beginners.

J.A. Thompson, *The Book of Jeremiah* (The New International Commentary on the Old Testament), Grand Rapids: William B. Eerdmans, 1980. A large-scale commentary, it is very much the echo of Bright's Anchor Bible volume and appears to be unaware of much recent scholarship on Jeremiah. It has some useful features and will serve well the cause of the historical reading of the text.

The major foreign-language commentaries include:

A. Aeschimann, *Le prophète Jérémie: Commentaire*, Paris: Editions Delachaux & Niestlé, 1959. Typical French rhetoric provides a conventional account of the text along the lines of Christian piety.

A. Condamin, *Le livre de Jérémie: Traduction et Commentaire* (Études Bibliques), 3rd edn, Paris: J. Gabalda & Cie, 1936. Very useful treatment of the text as poetry.

B. Duhm, *Das Buch Jeremia* (Kurzer Hand-Commentar zum Alten Testament XI), Tübingen: J.C.B. Mohr, 1901. Virtually a classic and one of the best commentaries available in any language on Jeremiah. Shrewd and insightful it will repay careful reading. An indispensable guide to understanding the book.

S. Herrmann, *Jeremia* (Biblischer Kommentar—Altes Testament XII/1), Neukirchen-Vluyn: Neukirchener Verlag, 1986. The first fascicle of what will prove to be the definitive and most comprehensive German commentary on Jeremiah.

H. Lamparter, *Prophet wider Willen: Der Prophet Jeremia* (Botschaft des Alten Testaments 20), Stuttgart: Calwer Verlag, 1964. A simple theological treatment of the text, with some useful insights and a clear organization of the book.

W. Rudolph, *Jeremia* (Handbuch zum Alten Testament I, 12), 3rd edn, Tübingen: J.C.B. Mohr, 1968. One of the best commentaries in German. It is an indispensable guide to understanding the Hebrew text published in BHS and represents a judicious balance of technical and exegetical treatments of the text. Follows the historical approach to the book, but includes a useful discussion of various opinions within the limits of space available to it.

P. Volz, *Der Prophet Jeremia* (Kommentar zum Alten Testament X), Leipzig: A. Deichertsche Verlagsbuchhandlung, 1922, 2nd edn, 1928. A very substantial commentary, with many valuable insights on the meaning of the text and useful treatments of textual problems. With Duhm and Rudolph it is an indispensable guide to the German interpretation of Jeremiah.

A. Weiser, *Das Buch des Propheten Jeremia* (Das Alte Testament Deutsch 20/21), 6th edn, Göttingen: Vandenhoeck & Ruprecht, 1969. Another major German commentary, taking a strongly theological view of Jeremiah. It has many interesting interpretations of individual texts in the book.

INDEX

INDEX OF BIBLICAL REFERENCES

INDEX OF AUTHORS